United States Government Accountability Office

Report to Congressional Requesters

I0448386

March 2013

INFORMATION SHARING

Additional Actions Could Help Ensure That Efforts to Share Terrorism-Related Suspicious Activity Reports Are Effective

This report was revised on March 26, 2013, to correct dates on pages 19 and 51 and correct an error on page 53.

GAO

Accountability ★ Integrity ★ Reliability

GAO-13-233

INFORMATION SHARING

Additional Actions Could Help Ensure That Efforts to Share Terrorism-Related Suspicious Activity Reports Are Effective

GAO
Accountability * Integrity * Reliability

Highlights

Highlights of GAO-13-233, a report to congressional requesters

Why GAO Did This Study

In 2007, DOJ and its federal partners developed the Nationwide Suspicious Activity Reporting Initiative to establish a capability to gather and share terrorism-related suspicious activity reports. GAO was asked to examine the initiative's progress and performance. This report addresses the extent to which (1) federal agencies have made progress in implementing the initiative, and what challenges, if any, remain; (2) the technical means used to collect and share reports overlap or duplicate each other; (3) training has met objectives and been completed; and (4) federal agencies are assessing the initiative's performance and results. GAO analyzed relevant documents and interviewed federal officials responsible for implementing the initiative and stakeholders from seven states (chosen based on their geographic location and other factors). The interviews are not generalizable but provided insight on progress and challenges.

What GAO Recommends

GAO recommends that DOJ implement formalized mechanisms to provide stakeholders feedback on the suspicious activity reports they submit, mitigate risks from supporting two systems to collect and share reports that may result in the FBI not receiving needed information, more fully assess if training for line officers meets their needs, and establish plans and time frames for implementing measures that assess the homeland security results the initiative has achieved. DOJ agreed with these recommendations and identified actions taken or planned to implement them.

View GAO-13-233. For more information, contact Eileen R. Larence at (202) 512-8777 or larencee@gao.gov.

What GAO Found

The Department of Justice (DOJ) has largely implemented the Nationwide Suspicious Activity Reporting Initiative among fusion centers—entities that serve as the focal point within a state for sharing and analyzing suspicious activity reports and other threat information. The state and local law enforcement officials GAO interviewed generally said the initiative's processes worked well, but that they could benefit from additional feedback from the Federal Bureau of Investigation (FBI) on how the reports they submit are used. The FBI has a feedback mechanism, but not all stakeholders were aware of it. Implementing formalized feedback mechanisms as part of the initiative could help stakeholders conduct accurate analyses of terrorism-related information, among other things.

The technical means that federal, state, and local entities use to collect and share terrorism-related suspicious activity reports—Shared Spaces servers that DOJ provides to most fusion centers and the FBI's eGuardian system—provide many overlapping or duplicative services. For example, both systems provide a national network for sharing the reports and tools to analyze them. The federal government is aware that duplication exists but supports both systems to enable fusion centers to control information on individuals, consistent with the centers' privacy requirements, and facilitate the FBI's investigative needs. However, the FBI was concerned that supporting two systems introduces risks that it will not receive all reports. For example, at the time of our review, many fusion centers were choosing not to automatically share all of their reports with the FBI's system—although they may have shared reports via phone or other means—and DOJ had not fully diagnosed why. In its March 2013 letter commenting on a draft of this report, DOJ stated that it had made progress on this issue. DOJ also had not formally tested the exchange of information between the two systems to ensure that the exchanges were complete. Taking additional steps to mitigate the risks that reports are not fully shared could help DOJ ensure that the FBI receives all information that can support investigations.

Stakeholders GAO interviewed generally reported that training fully or partially met objectives, such as making law enforcement more aware of the initiative. DOJ has mechanisms to assess the analyst training to help ensure that analysts have the information they need to review and share reports. However, DOJ had not fully assessed its training provided to officers on the front line, which could help ensure that officers receive sufficient information to be able to recognize terrorism-related suspicious activity. DOJ has provided training to executives at 77 of 78 fusion centers, about 2,000 fusion center analysts, and about 290,000 of the 800,000 line officers. DOJ is behind schedule in training the line officers but is taking actions to provide training to officers who have not yet received it.

DOJ and other agencies collect some data to assess the performance of the Nationwide Suspicious Activity Reporting Initiative—such as the number of reports submitted and resulting FBI investigations. These data show that stakeholders were increasingly submitting and using terrorism-related reports. However, DOJ had not yet established plans and time frames for implementing measures that assess the homeland security results achieved by the initiative and thus lacked a means for establishing accountability for implementing them.

_____ United States Government Accountability Office

Contents

Letter		1
	Background	4
	Almost All Fusion Centers and 53 Federal Agencies Are Participating in the NSI, but Feedback on the Use of SARs Could Be Enhanced	10
	Maintaining Two Systems That Duplicate the Function of Sharing ISE-SARs Introduces Risks That Have Not Been Fully Addressed	17
	Selected Stakeholders Reported Training to Date Generally Met Objectives, but Some Training Is behind Schedule and Has Not Been Fully Assessed	29
	ISE-SARs Are Increasingly Being Used to Support Investigations and Analysis, but the PMO Is Not Measuring the Homeland Security Results Achieved	33
	Conclusions	38
	Recommendations for Executive Action	39
	Agency Comments and Our Evaluation	40
Appendix I	Scope and Methodology	44
Appendix II	Functional Standard Terrorism-Related SAR Criteria Guidance	47
Appendix III	Federal Agencies Participating in the NSI	49
Appendix IV	Similar and Unique Services Provided by Shared Spaces and eGuardian	51
Appendix V	SAR Retention Policies in the FBI's eGuardian and Guardian Systems	53

Appendix VI	SAR Exchanges (Interoperability) among Shared Spaces, eGuardian, and Guardian	54
Appendix VII	Comments from the Department of Justice	56
Appendix VIII	Comments for the Department of Homeland Security	61
Appendix IX	GAO Contact and Staff Acknowledgments	62

Tables

Table 1: Nationwide Suspicious Activity Reporting Initiative Partners	4
Table 2: Nationwide Suspicious Activity Reporting Initiative Implementation	11
Table 3: Functional Standard ISE-SAR Criteria Guidance	47
Table 4: Similar Services Provided by Shared Spaces and eGuardian	51
Table 5: Unique Services Provided by Shared Spaces and eGuardian	52
Table 6: Retention Schedules for SARs in the FBI's eGuardian and Guardian Systems	53
Table 7: SAR Exchanges (Interoperability) among Shared Spaces, eGuardian, and Guardian	54

Figures

Figure 1: Nationwide Process for Collecting, Disseminating, and Utilizing Terrorism-related Suspicious Activity Reports	7
Figure 2: Similar and Unique Services Provided by Shared Spaces and eGuardian	19
Figure 3: Suspicious Activity Report (SAR) Exchanges (Interoperability) among Shared Spaces, eGuardian, and Guardian	27

Figure 4: Terrorism-Related Suspicious Activity Reports and Resulting FBI Investigations   34

Abbreviations

ACS	Automated Case Support
DHS	Department of Homeland Security
DOD	Department of Defense
DOJ	Department of Justice
FBI	Federal Bureau of Investigation
I&A	Office of Intelligence and Analysis
ISA IPC	Information Sharing and Access Interagency Policy Committee
ISE	Information Sharing Environment
IT	information technology
JTTF	Joint Terrorism Task Force
NARA	National Archives Records Administration
NSI	Nationwide Suspicious Activity Reporting Initiative
PMO	NSI Program Management Office
PM-ISE	Program Manager for the Information Sharing Environment
SAR	Suspicious Activity Report

March 13, 2013

Congressional Requesters

The attempted car bombing of Times Square in May 2010 was a planned terrorist attack that was foiled when street vendors alerted a New York Police Department officer after they spotted smoke coming from a vehicle. Two days later, federal agents arrested a 30-year-old Pakistan-born resident of Connecticut who subsequently pleaded guilty for attempting to carry out the attack. Every day, in the course of their duties, law enforcement officers at all levels of government—federal, state, local, and tribal—observe suspicious behaviors and receive information from concerned citizens, private security, and other government agencies, that could help detect, prevent, or deter a terrorist attack.

Consistent with provisions of law and executive branch policy addressing the need for information systems wherein state, local, and tribal law enforcement agencies could contribute potentially terrorism-related information, the federal government developed the Nationwide Suspicious Activity Reporting Initiative (NSI) in 2007.[1] The NSI establishes a nationwide capability to gather and share Suspicious Activity Reports (SAR) that have a potential nexus to terrorism.[2] These reports facilitate the identification and mitigation of potential terrorist threats as well as analysis to determine whether there are emerging patterns or trends suggesting such threats. In March 2010, the Department of Justice (DOJ) established the NSI Program Management Office (PMO) to support nationwide implementation of standardized processes for sharing terrorism-related SARs among federal, state, and local law enforcement agencies. To support NSI implementation, the PMO has facilitated the rollout of information-sharing technology and developed a training

---

[1] See, e.g., 6 U.S.C. § 485 (directing the President to create an information-sharing environment that, among other things, provides or supports a decentralized, distributed, and coordinated environment for sharing terrorism-related information), and Executive Office of the President, *National Strategy for Information Sharing: Successes and Challenges in Improving Terrorism-Related Information Sharing* (Washington D.C.: October 2007).

[2] In general, a SAR is official documentation of observed behavior reasonably indicative of preoperational planning related to terrorism or other criminal activity. The NSI facilitates the sharing of terrorism-related SARs.

strategy designed to enhance law enforcement professionals' ability to identify, report, evaluate, and share terrorism-related SARs.

We have designated the sharing of terrorism-related information as high risk because of the significant challenges the federal government faces in sharing this information in a timely, accurate, and useful manner.[3] The NSI is a key government program intended to address such challenges. You requested that we assess the NSI's progress and performance. In response to your request, this report addresses the extent to which

- DOJ and other federal entities have made progress in implementing the NSI, and what challenges remain, if any;

- the technical means that NSI stakeholders use to collect and share SARs overlap or duplicate each other and any risks this overlap or duplication may introduce;

- NSI training has met objectives, the PMO has assessed the training, and the training has been completed; and

- the PMO has assessed how well the NSI is working and the homeland security results it has achieved.

To address these objectives, we analyzed NSI programmatic documents, such as the NSI concept of operations and annual reports, and analyzed DOJ data—including data on NSI implementation, training, costs, and results—from the inception of the PMO in fiscal year 2010 through fiscal year 2012. We also interviewed officials from the Program Manager for the Information Sharing Environment (PM-ISE), DOJ, and the Department of Homeland Security (DHS) who are responsible for overseeing NSI efforts.[4] We obtained information from DOJ officials who manage the data about the steps taken to ensure their accuracy, and found the data to be sufficiently reliable for the purposes of this report.

---

[3]Terrorism-related information sharing remained a high-risk area for our February 2013 update. See GAO, *High-Risk Series: An Update*, GAO-13-283 (Washington, D.C.: Feb. 14, 2013) for the most recent update.

[4]The PM-ISE plans for, oversees implementation of, and manages the government-wide Information Sharing Environment (ISE)—an approach for sharing terrorism-related information that may include any method deemed necessary and appropriate. See 6 U.S.C. § 485(a)(3), (f).

In addition, to address the first three objectives, we interviewed nonprobability samples of officials from entities participating in the NSI, including officials from seven state or major urban area fusion centers—entities that serve as the focal point within a state for sharing and analyzing threat information.[5] We selected these centers based on their size, geographic location, and level of participation in the NSI, among other factors. At each center, we interviewed executives and analysts to obtain perspectives on NSI processes and related training they received. We also interviewed officials from each center who were familiar with their entities' systems for documenting and sharing terrorism-related SARs. Further, we interviewed Federal Bureau of Investigation (FBI) officials from field offices in proximity to the fusion centers we contacted who are responsible for investigating and analyzing SARs, as well as officials from five local law enforcement agencies in these locations who had taken NSI training. To obtain perspectives from participating federal agencies, we interviewed officials from the Federal Protective Service and the Bureau of Alcohol, Tobacco, Firearms and Explosives, which we selected based upon these agencies having a large number of officers who have received NSI training. Although the views of the individuals in our samples provide valuable insight into the implementation of the NSI, they are not generalizable to all federal, state, and local entities participating in the NSI.

We took additional steps to address the second, third, and fourth objectives regarding NSI technology, training, and results, respectively. To address the second objective, we analyzed DOJ documentation regarding the two primary systems that stakeholders use to collect, share, and analyze SARs—the PMO's Shared Spaces and the FBI's eGuardian system—such as user manuals and implementation guides. We compared the services of each system to determine the extent to which they overlap or were duplicative and assessed the extent to which DOJ followed best practices for ensuring that the systems effectively exchange information.[6] To address the third objective, we analyzed PMO documentation regarding training objectives, targets, and recipient

---

[5]Unlike a random sample, a nonprobability sample is more deliberatively chosen, meaning that some elements of the population being studied have either no chance or an unknown chance of being selected as part of the sample. Appendix I contains more information on the rationales we used to choose our samples.

[6]Best practices are included in DOJ, *The Department of Justice Systems Development Life Cycle Guidance Document* (Washington D.C.: January 2003*).

feedback mechanisms using leading practices for training programs.[7] To address the fourth objective, we assessed the PMO's plans for measuring the results the NSI has achieved using best practices for program management.[8] Appendix I contains more details about our scope and methodology.

We conducted this performance audit from February 2012 to March 2013 in accordance with generally accepted government auditing standards. Those standards require that we plan and perform the audit to obtain sufficient, appropriate evidence to provide a reasonable basis for our findings and conclusions based on our audit objectives. We believe that the evidence we obtained provides a reasonable basis for our findings and conclusions based on our audit objectives.

Background

NSI Partners

The NSI is a federal initiative that involves a collaborative effort of a number of federal, state, local, and private sector partners. Their roles are described in table 1.

Table 1: Nationwide Suspicious Activity Reporting Initiative Partners

Partner	Role
Program Manager for the Information Sharing Environment (PM-ISE)	• Plan for, oversee implementation of, and manage the Information Sharing Environment (ISE)—an approach for sharing terrorism-related information that may include any method deemed necessary and appropriate—in accordance with the Intelligence Reform and Terrorism Prevention Act of 2004, as amended.[a] • Developed Suspicious Activity Report (SAR) processes that eventually became the Nationwide Suspicious Activity Reporting Initiative (NSI), spending approximately $8 million on SAR-related activities from fiscal years 2006 through 2009. • Transferred management of the NSI to the Department of Justice (DOJ) after the administration designated DOJ as the executive agent for the program in December 2009. • Issues government-wide guidelines and standards for the management and operations of the NSI, and the ISE more generally.

[7]See, for example, GAO, *Human Capital: A Guide for Assessing Strategic Training and Development Efforts in the Federal Government,* GAO-04-546G (Washington D.C.: March 2004).

[8]The Project Management Institute, *The Standard for Program Management* © (Newton Square, PA: 2006).

Partner	Role
Program Management Office (PMO)	• Established within DOJ's Bureau of Justice Assistance in March 2010. • Responsible for implementing the NSI and assisting agencies with adopting compatible processes, policies, and standards that foster the sharing of SARs while ensuring that privacy, civil rights, and civil liberties are protected. • Developed training programs on identifying, reporting, evaluating, and sharing SARs to help prevent acts of terrorism. • Expended approximately $5.5 million in fiscal year 2010 and $4.1 million over fiscal years 2011 and 2012 to help implement the NSI.[b] Plans to spend up to an estimated $6.5 million in fiscal year 2013 to support NSI training and technology maintenance costs and enhancement, contingent upon available appropriations.
Federal Bureau of Investigation (FBI)	• Has jurisdiction over terrorism-related investigations and is responsible for investigating all terrorism-related SARs. • Established Joint Terrorism Task Forces (JTTF) to investigate terrorism-related activity in 103 cities nationwide, which include members from state and local law enforcement agencies as well as officials from other federal agencies, such as DHS and the Department of Defense (DOD). • Leads efforts to implement the NSI among federal entities. • Provides one of the technology platforms for the NSI (eGuardian), which is linked to the FBI's classified Guardian incident management system.
Department of Homeland Security (DHS)	• The Office of Intelligence and Analysis (I&A) is DHS's lead component with responsibilities for sharing terrorism-related information with all levels of government and the private sector. • I&A is responsible for implementing ISE initiatives at DHS, including the NSI, and coordinating DHS policy, training, and technical solutions related to the NSI. • I&A develops and distributes intelligence reports that are based in whole or in part on analysis of terrorism-related SARs shared through the NSI and provides training to fusion center personnel on SAR analysis methods and tools. DHS's Privacy Office and Office for Civil Rights and Civil Liberties also participate in NSI training. • DHS's Office of Infrastructure Protection and I&A work together to implement the NSI among owners and operators of critical infrastructure—assets and systems vital to the economy or health of the nation—such as oil refineries, dams, and telecommunications.[c]
Information Sharing and Access Interagency Policy Committee	• Established in July 2009 within the Executive Office of the President to identify information-sharing priorities, among other things. • Includes representation of participating ISE agencies—such as DOJ, DHS, and DOD—and provides oversight and guidance to the ISE. • Has a SAR Subcommittee that focuses on future high-level policies for federal SAR information sharing.
Fusion centers	• Focal points within states and localities for the receipt, analysis, gathering, and sharing of terrorism and other threat-related information, including SARs. • Generally owned and operated by state and local entities—with support from federal agencies—that collectively provide resources, expertise, and information to detect, prevent, and respond to criminal and terrorist activity. • Review SARs contributed by state and local entities within their jurisdictions—such as law enforcement agencies—to determine whether they are terrorism-related and should be shared through the NSI. • Analyze SARs and develop relevant products to disseminate to other NSI stakeholders to help identify and address immediate and emerging threats.

Partner	Role
State, local, and tribal law enforcement and hometown security partners	• State, local, and tribal law enforcement agencies gather information regarding behaviors and incidents that may have a nexus to terrorism. The NSI creates a standardized process for collecting and sharing this information. • Hometown security partners—such as critical infrastructure owners and operators, firefighters, emergency medical service providers, and private sector security professionals—also have routine duties that position them to observe and report suspicious behaviors.

Source: GAO analysis of PM-ISE, DOJ, and DHS documents and interviews.

[a]See Pub. L. No. 108-458, § 1016, 118 Stat. 3638, 3664-70 (2004) (codified as amended at 6 U.S.C. § 485).

[b]Funding amounts do not include federal staff that support the PMO, which are provided by DOJ's Bureau of Justice Assistance, the FBI, DHS, and the PM-ISE. Staffing levels ranged from a total of 6.5 full-time equivalents in fiscal year 2010 to 4.75 full-time equivalents in fiscal year 2012. The $4.1 million expended in fiscal years 2011 and 2012 was from amounts appropriated in 2011.

[c]Consistent with Homeland Security Presidential Directive/HSPD-7 (Dec. 17, 2003), DHS has identified 18 critical infrastructure sectors: Food and Agriculture; Banking and Finance; Chemical; Commercial Facilities; Communications; Critical Manufacturing; Dams; Defense Industrial Base; Emergency Services; Energy; Government Facilities; Healthcare and Public Heath; Information Technology; National Monuments and Icons; Nuclear Reactors, Materials and Waste; Postal and Shipping; Transportation Systems; and Water. Presidential Policy Directive/PPD-21, issued February 12, 2013, revoked HSPD-7 and realigns the 18 sectors into 16 critical infrastructure sectors but also provides that plans developed pursuant to HSPD-7 shall remain in effect until specifically revoked or superseded.

Nationwide SAR Process

The NSI builds upon established, but largely ad hoc, processes that law enforcement agencies have used for years to collect information on suspicious activities. In 2008, the PM-ISE—in coordination with the Executive Office of the President and state, local, and tribal partners—established a "Functional Standard" that defines processes for collecting and sharing SARs that have a potential nexus to terrorism. Among other things, the Functional Standard includes a set of behavior-based criteria for analysts to use to help them determine if a SAR has a potential nexus to terrorism—such as a breach or attempted intrusion, expressed or implied threat, or cyber attack—and should be shared with other NSI participants.[9] SARs that are determined to have a potential nexus to terrorism pursuant to the Functional Standard are known as ISE-SARs.[10]

[9]PM-ISE, *ISE Functional Standard: Suspicious Activity Reporting, Version 1.5*, ISE-FS-200 (Washington D.C.: May 21, 2009). Appendix II contains additional information on the Functional Standard.

[10]According to FBI officials, the FBI uses the criteria in the eGuardian Privacy Impact Assessment (dated November 25, 2008) and the FBI's Domestic Investigations and Operations Guide to determine if SARs have a potential nexus to terrorism. The officials said that these criteria are generally consistent with the Functional Standard and the FBI and PMO are taking steps to further harmonize the criteria.

The PMO, FBI, and other entities further clarified the business processes associated with sharing ISE-SARs in an April 2012 two-page bulletin. Figure 1 outlines the process for collecting, disseminating, and utilizing SARs.

Figure 1: Nationwide Process for Collecting, Disseminating, and Utilizing Terrorism-related Suspicious Activity Reports

Observe   Report   Review   Disseminate   Analyze/assess

 Observation of suspicious activity
Initial observer may be a private citizen, a representative of a private sector partner, a government official, or a law enforcement officer.

 Suspicious activity reported to a law enforcement agency that performs local review
Suspicious activity is eventually reported to a local law enforcement agency or a local, regional, or national office of a Federal agency. The information is reviewed within these agencies in accordance with departmental policies and procedures.

 Suspicious Activity Report (SAR) is sent to either a fusion center or the FBI, which reviews the SAR against the Functional Standard[a]
The local or federal agency prepares a SAR and provides it to its designated fusion center or the FBI, where trained analysts review the SAR and compare it with criteria outlined in the Functional Standard to determine if it has a potential nexus to terrorism.

 Terrorism-related SAR submitted to Shared Spaces or eGuardian for broader dissemination
If a SAR is determined to have a potential nexus to terrorism, it becomes a terrorism-related SAR (an ISE-SAR) and is electronically submitted into Shared Spaces and/or eGuardian, where it is accessible to authorized law enforcement and intelligence personnel.

 Stakeholders use ISE-SAR for investigative and analytic purposes
FBI personnel perform an assessment on the ISE-SAR to determine whether or not to take further action—such as opening an investigation. Fusion centers, the FBI, and DHS use the ISE-SAR to create analytic products.

Source: GAO analysis of PM-ISE and DOJ documents; Art Explosion (clip art).

[a]According to FBI officials, the FBI uses the criteria in the eGuardian Privacy Impact Assessment (dated November 25, 2008) and the FBI's Domestic Investigations and Operations Guide to determine if SARs have a potential nexus to terrorism. The officials said that these criteria are generally consistent with the Functional Standard and the FBI and PMO are taking steps to further harmonize the criteria.

Systems Used to Share ISE-SARs

The NSI leverages technologies—the ISE Shared Spaces and the FBI's eGuardian system—to facilitate the collection, dissemination, and utilization of ISE-SARs. Previously, federal, state, local, and tribal law enforcement entities generally stored SARs at the local agency level and used nonstandard methods—such as telephone, fax, or e-mail—to share SARs with the FBI. Law enforcement entities may continue to use these methods for submitting SARs to the FBI, but the development of Shared Spaces and eGuardian allows for electronic submission, sharing, and access to ISE-SARs for analysis nationwide. Shared Spaces and eGuardian were created during the same time frame (2007 to 2009), and both systems were first implemented in 2008.

The PMO has provided Shared Spaces servers to most fusion centers across the country. These servers allow centers to store ISE-SARs locally and retain ownership and exclusive control over modifying and deleting them, consistent with state laws and regulations and fusion center policies designed to protect privacy.[11] ISE-SARs that are modified or deleted in a fusion center's information system are subsequently modified or deleted in its Shared Spaces server through a regularly scheduled update process. A search tool called the NSI Federated Search allows fusion centers to use a single query to view ISE-SARs located on Shared Spaces servers across the country.

The FBI's eGuardian system is an unclassified part of the FBI's secret-level counterterrorism incident management system (Guardian) that is used to support the FBI's investigative needs. eGuardian was created to bridge the gap between the classified Guardian system and the sensitive but unclassified law enforcement environment. eGuardian's Privacy Impact Assessment notes that all SARs submitted to eGuardian remain the property and under the control of the submitting agency. All ISE-SARs that fusion centers submit to eGuardian are forwarded to Guardian.[12] The

---

[11]PMO officials noted that Shared Spaces could also be used to share other types of criminal information, such as gang-related data. The PM-ISE has recommended that DOJ examine the potential for using Shared Spaces to share critical information on other priority threats and crimes. The PM-ISE noted that, as of December 2012, DOJ had not yet submitted an implementation plan for such an approach.

[12]When law enforcement agencies submit SARs through eGuardian, personnel at the area fusion center or the FBI's "eFusion center" vet the SAR against the Functional Standard or an equivalent standard before the SAR is disseminated within eGuardian for broader viewing.

GAO-13-233 Suspicious Activity Reporting

FBI may also send unclassified information from Guardian to eGuardian. eGuardian has a search tool that allows users to view eGuardian ISE-SARs submitted by users nationwide. To make ISE-SARs in eGuardian searchable and viewable to Federated Search users, the FBI maintains an eGuardian Shared Spaces server and forwards all eGuardian ISE-SARs to this server.[13]

Privacy and Civil Liberties

Federal, state, and local agencies have taken steps to help address the protection of privacy, civil rights, and civil liberties during the nationwide SAR process. For example, the NSI definition of a SAR was developed with input from several privacy, civil rights, and civil liberties advocacy groups. In addition, the Functional Standard uses behavior-based criteria for determining whether an activity has a potential nexus to terrorism—such as attempting to enter a restricted area or protected site—and notes that SARs should not be based solely on First Amendment-protected activities or factors, such as race, ethnicity, or religion. The Functional Standard also defines "personal information" as any information that may be used to identify individuals, such as an address, Social Security number, or license plate, and identifies which data elements within SARs may contain such personal information. The Functional Standard further recognizes that laws that prohibit or otherwise limit the sharing of personal information vary considerably among federal, state, local, and tribal levels.

To facilitate lawful information sharing, the technical means for sharing information nationwide—Shared Spaces and eGuardian—both have capabilities that enable agencies to safeguard personal information. Furthermore, the NSI developed a Privacy Framework that fusion centers and federal agencies who share ISE-SARs through the NSI must adopt prior to participating. Specifically, the framework requires that participating entities (1) have an approved privacy policy in place that meets minimum requirements, such as ensuring data quality and security, prior to sharing ISE-SARs through the NSI; (2) use the Functional Standard to vet and determine if SARs have a potential nexus to terrorism; and (3) incorporate the delivery of privacy training.

---

[13]Additional information on which entities use Shared Spaces servers and which use eGuardian is discussed later in this report.

DHS has also supported fusion centers in their self-initiated efforts to perform peer-to-peer audits to help ensure their continued adherence to SAR privacy protections, among other things. According to DHS officials, as of December 2012, fusion centers had completed 20 peer-to-peer privacy audits. The officials noted that some centers choose to conduct their own internal reviews or they are conducted by their parent agencies. In fiscal year 2013, the PMO plans to introduce a self-audit process for fusion centers to review their submission of ISE-SARs to ensure they adhere to the Functional Standard.

Almost All Fusion Centers and 53 Federal Agencies Are Participating in the NSI, but Feedback on the Use of SARs Could Be Enhanced

Most fusion centers and federal law enforcement agencies can now share ISE-SARs through the NSI. Participants we interviewed generally said that the NSI process is working well, but some state and local officials said that additional feedback on how the SARs are used could help them better contribute to the NSI. FBI officials we interviewed were concerned that fusion center processes for reviewing SARs may prevent them from receiving all SARs in a timely manner. The PMO and FBI are taking steps to revise NSI guidance to address the FBI's concerns.

NSI Stakeholders Have Established the Capability to Share ISE-SARs at 74 of 78 Fusion Centers and 53 Federal Agencies

The PMO has largely implemented the NSI at fusion centers, which in turn allows all law enforcement agencies within the fusion centers' jurisdictions to begin providing ISE-SARs as part of the NSI. The PMO and DHS have also begun training other homeland security partners—such as critical infrastructure owners and operators and emergency medical technicians—to identify and report terrorism-related SARs to the NSI. FBI officials said they have reached out to all federal departments and are implementing the NSI at agencies that have law enforcement or military force protection personnel that would be in a position to observe suspicious activity.[14] The officials said they are determining if there are any additional agencies that should participate. Table 2 contains additional information on NSI implementation.

---

[14]The federal agencies participating in the NSI include independent federal agencies and government corporations.

GAO-13-233 Suspicious Activity Reporting

Table 2: Nationwide Suspicious Activity Reporting Initiative Implementation

Entity type	Participation requirements	Participation status
Fusion centers	Technical requirements for sharing and analyzing Suspicious Activity Reports (SAR): • obtain access to eGuardian (obtaining a Shared Spaces server is optional); and • obtain access to the NSI Federated Search tool. Policy requirements to protect privacy, civil rights, and civil liberties: • enter into a participation agreement with the Nationwide Suspicious Activity Reporting Initiative (NSI) Program Management Office (PMO); • have at least one analyst trained to vet against the Functional Standard, enter into eGuardian or Shared Spaces, and analyze SARs; • have an approved privacy policy in place; and • have an approved site plan that describes the center's procedures and technology for implementing the SAR process.	According to PMO officials, as of February 2013, 74 of 78 fusion centers had established the capability to share SARs: • 72 of 78 fusion centers had implemented all technical and policy requirements (54 fusion centers also had a Shared Spaces server); • 2 fusion centers had implemented the technical requirements required to share SARs but had not completed the policy requirements; • 2 fusion centers intended to participate in the NSI but had not yet completed the technical or policy requirements; and • 2 fusion centers had opted to not participate in the NSI;[a]
State, local, and tribal law enforcement	No requirements are set for state, local, and tribal law enforcement agencies to participate in the NSI.	According to PMO data, as of November 2012, more than 14,200 local law enforcement agencies in 46 states; Washington, D.C.; and 2 U.S. territories had the capability to share ISE-SARs through the 74 fusion centers where the NSI is being implemented.
Hometown security partners	No specific requirements are set for hometown security partners to be able to report SARs. The PMO and DHS are working with key critical infrastructure and public safety associations to launch an outreach campaign to help provide training to hometown security partners.	• As of February 2013, more than 52,800 hometown security partners had received training. • As of May 2012, 6 of 18 DHS-recognized critical infrastructure sectors were able to submit SAR data through DHS's Homeland Security Information Network, a secure web-based portal for information sharing. • PMO officials said they plan to introduce maritime sector–focused SAR training in fiscal year 2013.

GAO-13-233 Suspicious Activity Reporting

Entity type	Participation requirements	Participation status
Federal agencies	Technical and policy requirements to participate in the NSI: • obtain access to eGuardian, • receive an executive-level briefing, • enter into a participation agreement with the PMO to document participation in the NSI, • establish a SAR protocol that describes the process for reviewing and submitting SARs, • adhere to a privacy policy, and • complete training for frontline officers and analysts. Federal agencies have the option of obtaining a Shared Spaces server.	According to the FBI, as of November 2012: • 27 federal agencies and the Department of Defense had met all technical and policy requirements; and • 26 federal agencies had met all requirements except for completing analyst training.[b] • DHS and the Department of Transportation had decided to obtain Shared Spaces servers. All other federal agencies are using eGuardian as their means of sharing SARs.

Source: GAO analysis of DOJ documents and interviews with DOJ officials.

[a]PMO officials said these fusion centers opted not to participate in the NSI and therefore do not enter SARs into Shared Spaces or eGuardian because of state legal restrictions on sharing SARs in this manner.

[b]Appendix III provides a list of the 53 federal agencies participating in the NSI.

Selected State and Local Participants Reported the SAR Process Generally Worked Well, but More Feedback on the Use of SARs Could Help them Improve Reporting

Officials from 6 of the 7 fusion centers and 4 of the 5 local law enforcement agencies we interviewed said that the NSI process for vetting and submitting potentially terrorism-related SARs generally worked well for them.[15] The officials cited a number of benefits from their participation in the NSI. For example, they reported that

- having the ability to view ISE-SARs from across the nation has allowed their fusion center to conduct analysis to identify trends of concern and potential threats,

- an increase in the quality of ISE-SARs has led to better information on potential terrorist threats,

---

[15]Officials from the remaining fusion center said they did not know if the process was working well. An official from the remaining local agency said that the process was not working well and that the agency needed additional information to ensure that all officers know to whom to provide SAR information.

- the Functional Standard has led to a common understanding of what terrorism-related ISE-SARs are and has helped protect privacy and civil liberties when sharing ISE-SARs, and

- officers have a better understanding of suspicious activities that may be indicative of terrorism and the importance of reporting SARs.

These views were consistent with national law enforcement organizations' views—such as those of the International Association of Chiefs of Police and the Major Cities Chiefs Association—which have supported the creation of the NSI and its implementation nationwide.

Fusion center and local law enforcement agency officials we interviewed generally said that receiving additional feedback on the SARs they submit—such as whether the FBI has received the SARs, whether the FBI is investigating the SARs, or what the outcomes of any investigations are—would help them better contribute to the NSI. Specifically, executives from all 7 of the fusion centers, analysts from 6 of the 7 fusion centers, and officials from all 5 local law enforcement agencies we interviewed said that receiving feedback on the outcome of SARs they submit was important. They noted, for instance, that feedback reinforces that there is value in reporting, helps to identify what threats exist in their area so that they know what to look for, helps to ensure their SARs are accurate, and encourages officers to continue reporting.[16]

The FBI has established a mechanism to provide feedback on ISE-SARs through eGuardian, but not all of the stakeholders we interviewed were aware of or had access to this mechanism. Specifically, the FBI uses eGuardian to inform stakeholders of whether it has determined through an initial assessment if the ISE-SAR has (1) a potential nexus to terrorism and warrants an investigation, (2) an inconclusive nexus to terrorism, or (3) no nexus to terrorism. FBI officials noted that eGuardian also provides the SAR submitter details about when the SAR was received by the FBI; which FBI field office is investigating the SAR; and contact information if the fusion center or state, local, or tribal law enforcement officials want additional information about the SAR. However, not all stakeholders use eGuardian and thus would not see this feedback. For example, while all fusion centers participating in the NSI have access to eGuardian, they

---

[16]Analysts from the remaining fusion center said that feedback was not that important because their job is just to make sure that the FBI receives the information.

may choose to use the Federated Search tool rather than eGuardian to review ISE-SARs and conduct analysis. Local law enforcement agencies are eligible to receive eGuardian accounts, but they do not need one to participate in the NSI, as they can provide SAR information to fusion centers or the FBI through other means, such as phone calls or e-mails. Officials from 3 of the 7 fusion centers we interviewed said they did not use eGuardian to review ISE-SAR data and officials from 2 of the 5 law enforcement agencies we interviewed said they did not have an eGuardian account. Moreover, executives and analysts from 4 of the 7 fusion centers we interviewed were not aware that this feedback existed.

To help ensure that NSI participants receive feedback, the PM-ISE recommended in February 2010 that the PMO formalize NSI feedback mechanisms, but the PMO has not yet done so. Specifically, formalized feedback mechanisms were to ensure that at a minimum (1) organizations that receive SARs—such as fusion centers and the FBI— notify entities that submit SARs when information they provide is designated as a ISE-SAR and shared, and (2) fusion center or FBI personnel notify all NSI participants when further evidence leads them to determine that a ISE-SAR should no longer be designated as being terrorism-related so that the original information does not continue to be used as the basis for analysis or action.[17] Discontinuing use of such SARs, when applicable, may also address concerns related to the protection of privacy and civil liberties. According to PMO officials, formalized feedback mechanisms have not been established because they thought it would be best to let each fusion center determine if and how to elicit and provide feedback. However, as our work indicated, most of the fusion center officials we interviewed had not established such mechanisms and were not aware that the FBI provided feedback.

Standards for Internal Control in the Federal Government notes that management should ensure there are adequate means of communicating with, and obtaining information from, external stakeholders that may have a significant impact on achieving program objectives.[18] Implementing formalized NSI feedback mechanisms—which could include leveraging

---

[17]PM-ISE, *Nationwide Suspicious Activity Reporting Initiative Status Report* (Washington D.C.: February 2010).

[18]GAO, *Internal Control: Standards for Internal Control in the Federal Government*, GAO/AIMD-00-21.3.1 (Washington, D.C.: November 1999).

existing mechanisms such as those in eGuardian—and communicating these mechanisms to stakeholders could help ensure that NSI stakeholders receive the information they need to enforce SAR policies designed to protect privacy considerations, maintain situational awareness, conduct accurate analyses, or motivate personnel to continue to report SARs.

Selected Federal Participants Reported the NSI Process Generally Worked Well; Agencies Are Addressing FBI Concerns about Potentially Not Receiving Some Information

Officials from five of the seven JTTFs we interviewed, the Federal Protective Service, and the Bureau of Alcohol, Tobacco, Firearms and Explosives said that the NSI process to vet and submit SARs generally worked well for them.[19] For example, officials from four of the JTTFs said that the process had helped them receive more SARs from state and local agencies. Further, none of the JTTF officials believed that the NSI process had led to an overload of nonrelevant information. Officials from the Federal Protective Service and the Bureau of Alcohol, Tobacco, Firearms and Explosives said that the NSI has contributed to an increase in the number of ISE-SARs they submit.

However, FBI officials from headquarters and all seven JTTFs we interviewed said that they had concerns that the FBI may not be receiving all available terrorism-related information because some fusion centers may share only ISE-SARs with the FBI—that is, SARs that have been determined to have a potential nexus to terrorism consistent with the Functional Standard criteria. They explained that the Functional Standard criteria are not as broad as the FBI's guidelines for investigating terrorism-related information.[20] For example, FBI headquarters officials said that certain terrorism-related activities—such as those related to terrorist financing, known terrorism subject location, and past terrorism event information—currently are not among the behavior-based criteria in the Functional Standard but would meet the FBI's guidelines. FBI officials

---

[19]Officials from one of the two remaining JTTFs said they did not know if the NSI process was working well, and officials from the other JTTF said the NSI process was not working well because they were not aware of it. We interviewed both line officers and analysts from the Federal Protective Service and the Bureau of Alcohol, Tobacco, Firearms and Explosives. One bureau analyst we met with did not know if the process was working well. One Federal Protective Service line officer said that the process is not working well because law enforcement officials had multiple ways to report SARs.

[20]FBI investigative criteria are documented in its *Domestic Investigations and Operations Guide.*

did not have readily available data on the extent to which SARs that do not meet the Functional Standard criteria are provided to the FBI. Officials from four of the JTTFs we interviewed said that they had coordinated with the fusion centers in their jurisdictions to inform the fusion centers that they should provide all potentially terrorism-related information and not just ISE-SARs that met the Functional Standard. Officials from one JTTF noted that the state's fusion center had provided approximately 270 suspicious incident reports containing potentially terrorism-related information from June 2011 to October 2012, but only about 10 percent of them met the Functional Standard and were entered into Shared Spaces by the fusion center.

The extent to which the fusion center officials we interviewed said they provide SARs that did not meet the Functional Standard to the FBI varied. Officials from 3 fusion centers said that they would always or most of the time provide SARs that did not meet the Functional Standard to the FBI; officials from 3 fusion centers said they would provide these SARs some of the time or occasionally based on their professional judgment; and officials from 1 fusion center said that they would never provide these SARs to the FBI, in accordance with the fusion center's privacy policy. PMO and FBI officials said that they were working together to address this issue and develop a new version of the Functional Standard that is intended to harmonize the criteria that the FBI and fusion centers use to share ISE-SARs within the NSI. PMO officials said that the new Functional Standard will also provide guidance on sharing SARs with the FBI that do not meet the Functional Standard to help ensure that the FBI receives all relevant terrorism-related information while still protecting privacy and civil liberties. As of November 2012, PMO officials said that the draft of the new Functional Standard was completed and was awaiting PM-ISE and Information Sharing and Access Interagency Policy Committee (ISA IPC) review and approval. In the meantime, PMO officials said that when fusion center personnel contact them with questions about whether or not to share a SAR, the officials advise the personnel to share the information with the FBI.

Officials from FBI headquarters and four JTTFs we interviewed also had concerns that fusion centers may be taking steps to investigate SARs—such as interviewing the individuals engaged in suspicious activity or who witnessed suspicious activity—before providing the SARs to the FBI.[21]

---

[21]Officials from the other three JTTFs we met with did not raise this concern.

Officials from 3 of the 7 fusion centers we interviewed said that they may do investigative work as part of their vetting process.[22] An official from one of these fusion centers explained that conducting some preliminary investigative work as part of the vetting process allows the center to better determine if the incident should be reported as an ISE-SAR. However, according to FBI officials, by conducting independent investigative work, fusion centers could disrupt ongoing FBI investigations or inappropriately dismiss a SAR and not provide relevant terrorism-related information to the FBI. PMO officials said that they have limited ability to control investigative procedures at state and local agencies, but the PMO's analytical training materials note that the vetting process should not include investigating. Further, PMO officials said that they plan to make a training video available in March 2013 that will further clarify that investigative work is not an appropriate part of vetting procedure.

Maintaining Two Systems That Duplicate the Function of Sharing ISE-SARs Introduces Risks That Have Not Been Fully Addressed

The NSI leverages the ISE Shared Spaces and the FBI's eGuardian system to collect and share ISE-SARs. The two systems have overlapping goals and offer duplicative services, but also have some unique features. The federal government has decided to support both systems to meet users' differing needs. However, maintaining two systems introduces the risk that the FBI may not be able to review all potential terrorist threats because many fusion centers have decided not to automatically share all of their ISE-SARs with eGuardian, and the interconnection between the systems has not been fully tested. The PMO and FBI have taken steps to mitigate these risks, but they have not been fully addressed.

---

[22]The fusion centers that said they conducted investigative work were not always in the same jurisdictions as the JTTFs that raised concerns about such actions.

Shared Spaces and eGuardian Both Serve Fusion Centers and Provide Many Duplicative Services

As of November 2012, a total of 74 fusion centers had the capability to share ISE-SARs, of which 54 centers had a Shared Spaces server and all 74 centers had eGuardian accounts.[23] In general, fusion centers use Shared Spaces servers to store ISE-SAR information locally and authorize other fusion centers to view their ISE-SARs, and use eGuardian to share ISE-SARs with the FBI and other eGuardian users. Fusion centers have the option to submit ISE-SARs to Shared Spaces only, to eGuardian only, or to both Shared Spaces and eGuardian. According to PMO officials, fusion centers that submit ISE-SARs only to Shared Spaces provide them to the FBI through other means—such as telephone, e-mail, or fax. ISE-SARs that users submit only to eGuardian are forwarded to the FBI's Shared Spaces server, where they are accessible to users of Shared Spaces. Fusion centers provided different reasons for choosing to use one or both systems. For example, officials at 1 fusion center said they chose to use Shared Spaces because, among other things, it offered them the ability to remove ISE-SARs at their discretion—meaning that once they remove an ISE-SAR from their server, it may no longer be viewed by another party through the Federated Search—which is required for them to comply with their fusion center's privacy policy. Officials at another center said they chose eGuardian because FBI officials visited them and explained the system before they were made aware of Shared Spaces.

We have previously reported that overlap occurs when programs have similar goals, devise similar strategies and activities to achieve those goals, or target similar users; and duplication occurs when two or more agencies or programs are engaged in the same activities or provide the same services to the same beneficiaries. Since their creation, both Shared Spaces and eGuardian have provided many of the same services, including a nationwide network for sharing ISE-SARs and capabilities to analyze them for patterns and trends. Shared Spaces and eGuardian also contain much of the same information. Figure 2 shows the services that both Shared Spaces and eGuardian provide, as well as services that are unique to each system.

---

[23]To participate in the NSI, fusion centers are required to have access to eGuardian and the NSI Federated Search. Having access to eGuardian enables them to submit ISE-SARs to, and review and analyze ISE-SARs within, eGuardian. Having access to the NSI Federated Search enables them to review and analyze ISE-SARs in Shared Spaces. Many fusion centers have also chosen to obtain a Shared Spaces server, which enables them to contribute ISE-SARs to Shared Spaces.

Figure 2: Similar and Unique Services Provided by Shared Spaces and eGuardian

Mouse over the colored boxes for information on how the system implements the service. For readers of print copies, see appendix IV.

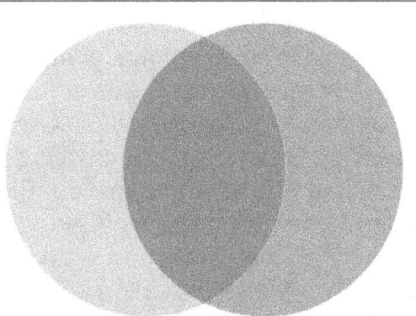

Shared Spaces	Services provided by both	eGuardian
Control over who can add information to ISE-SARs	Access to submit ISE-SARs into nationwide network	Ability for users other than the original ISE-SAR submitter to supplement ISE-SAR information
Control over who can download ISE-SARs	Access to review and analyze ISE-SARs others have submitted	Ability to access FBI feedback on ISE-SARs
Greater control of the retention periods of ISE-SARs	Ability to share ISE-SAR information with the other system	Ability to download ISE-SARs
Ability to restrict certain data elements from broader view	Search and analysis tools	Fixed retention schedules for ISE-SARs in eGuardian and Guardian
Ability to perform a federated search over all ISE-SARs in the NSI	Ability to submit ISE-SARs to FBI JTTFs and to Guardian (the FBI's classified counterterrorism incident management system)	Ability to share information with the FBI but not with other users of eGuardian or Shared Spaces
	Ability to remove ISE-SARs from the NSI on demand	Ability to request coordination with the FBI

Legend

SAR	Suspicious Activity Report
ISE-SAR	Information Sharing Environment SAR (terrorism-related SAR)
JTTF	Joint Terrorism Task Force
NSI	Nationwide SAR Initiative

Source: GAO analysis of DOJ documents and interviews.

[a]In commenting on a draft of this report, FBI officials noted that in February 2013, the FBI implemented a new feature in eGuardian that allows fusion centers to directly and electronically remove their ISE-SARs.

According to PM-ISE officials, Shared Spaces was created in part based on fusion centers' feedback indicating that having control over the ISE-SARs they submit was essential for complying with state and local laws, regulations, and policies that are intended to protect the privacy rights of individuals in their jurisdiction. The officials added that eGuardian was not sufficient for providing that control. For example, the officials explained that they received feedback from fusion centers that the FBI process of automatically uploading ISE-SARs from eGuardian into the FBI's classified Guardian system limits fusion centers' control over their submitted ISE-SAR information. PMO officials also noted the importance of the "read-only" nature of Shared Spaces as a significant privacy protection. They explained that ISE-SAR contributors have proprietary rights over their information and expose it to others only upon the basis of another's query for viewing purposes—downloading, deleting, or otherwise modifying information in Shared Spaces is not possible. DHS officials added that this read-only feature safeguards against amassing copies of datasets that may be inaccurate or out of date.

As a result, PMO officials said that Shared Spaces and eGuardian should both continue to exist since Shared Spaces provides fusion centers with exclusive control over the ISE-SARs they submit and eGuardian serves the FBI's investigative needs. The officials noted that state and local leaders have endorsed the Shared Spaces model as the framework for sharing ISE-SARs among state and local entities.

FBI officials recognized that some fusion centers may prefer to use Shared Spaces as their primary means of sharing ISE-SARs and said that the FBI is satisfied with this arrangement as long as ISE-SARs in Shared Spaces are automatically shared with eGuardian.[24] However, in the FBI's opinion, it would not be cost effective for fusion centers—for which eGuardian fully meets their ISE-SAR sharing needs and is a center's preferred approach—to switch to Shared Spaces. The FBI noted that approximately half of the fusion centers use eGuardian to share ISE-SARs, and do so at no cost to the fusion centers.

Determining whether the federal government was investing significant resources in maintaining both systems proved difficult. The FBI provided

---

[24]We discuss the automatic sharing of ISE-SARs between Shared Spaces and eGuardian later in this report.

costs for the overall Guardian system, but it did not separate the costs for the eGuardian component.[25] According to PMO officials, federal costs for the development, operations, and maintenance of Shared Spaces totaled about $600,000 from fiscal year 2010 through fiscal year 2012, and are expected to total about $1.26 million for fiscal years 2013 through 2015. The PMO did not know the costs that fusion centers and other owners of Shared Spaces servers bear, but had heard anecdotally that these costs were not significant. Although the PMO initially provided Shared Spaces servers to fusion centers, PMO officials said that the federal government does not plan to pay any replacement costs for them and that given the expected 7-year useful life of the servers, any cost estimate would be speculative. The officials noted that state and local entities would pay any replacement costs.

The PM-ISE is aware that Shared Spaces and eGuardian duplicate many services but said that both systems are currently needed to meet users' differing needs. The PM-ISE noted that representatives from the PM-ISE, DOJ, DHS, FBI, and Office of the Director of National Intelligence who serve on the ISA IPC[26] have participated in efforts that formally recognize the two-system approach, such as the unified message to NSI stakeholders that we discuss later in this report. We have similarly reported that in some instances of overlap or duplication, it may be appropriate for multiple agencies or entities to be involved in the same programmatic or policy area because of the nature or magnitude of the federal effort, and that many of the meaningful results that the federal government seeks to achieve require the coordinated efforts of more than one federal agency and often more than one sector and level of government.

---

[25]Costs associated with Guardian are available on the federal information technology (IT) Dashboard—a website that enables the general public and other stakeholders to view details of federal IT investments.

[26]The ISA IPC—within the Executive Office of the President—has a SAR Subcommittee that is responsible for resolving related interagency disputes, among other things.

Maintaining Both Shared Spaces and eGuardian Introduces Risks, Which Have Not Been Fully Addressed

Twenty-six Fusion Centers Were Not Always Simultaneously Submitting ISE-SARs to Shared Spaces and eGuardian

The FBI expressed concern that fusion centers were not always simultaneously submitting ISE-SARs to eGuardian when they submitted them to Shared Spaces, and DOJ was not fully aware of the reasons why. According to a November 2011 document, DOJ's Bureau of Justice Assistance and the FBI believed there were upwards of 1,000 ISE-SARs that were in Shared Spaces but not eGuardian.[27] The document noted that that this was an unacceptable risk to the country because the FBI needs to receive what may be time-sensitive information to ensure ISE-SARs can be tracked and accountability processes are in place for analysis and investigative purposes. According to FBI officials, by November 2012, the FBI and fusion centers had subsequently accounted for 700 to 800 of the 1,000 ISE-SARs, but could not confirm that the remaining 200 to 300 ISE-SARs were provided to the FBI.

To address the FBI's concern, in November 2011, the Deputy Attorney General issued a memo to fusion center directors that was intended to ensure that all fusion centers that had a Shared Spaces server implement an electronic capability to simultaneously submit ISE-SARs to both Shared Spaces and eGuardian. The memo noted that the FBI has the lead responsibility for investigating terrorism threats and eGuardian is the only federal system designed to accept and track leads for counterterrorism investigations. In December 2011, the Associate Attorney General and the Deputy Director of the FBI sent a memo to the Deputy Attorney General that outlined steps the PMO and FBI would take to ensure that terrorism-related information collected within the NSI is reported to the FBI through eGuardian, which included the following:[28]

---

[27]The FBI has access to ISE-SARs in Shared Spaces through the Federated Search, but FBI headquarters officials said that it is difficult to systematically try to match ISE-SARs in eGuardian to the ISE-SARs in Shared Spaces because Shared Spaces does not allow users to search for ISE-SARs that were entered during a specific time frame.

[28]The Associate Attorney General advises and assists the Attorney General and the Deputy Attorney General in formulating and implementing departmental policies and programs.

- A 90-day period wherein if a user chose to submit an ISE-SAR to Shared Spaces but not eGuardian, the user was to provide an explanation as to why that user chose to do so.

- During this period, the PMO was to conduct weekly audits to determine which fusion centers were not sharing ISE-SARs with eGuardian and their reasons why. The PMO and FBI would then follow up with those centers to identify the nature of the issues (e.g., technical, legal, or policy-based) and the best way to address them.

- After this period, fusion centers were to no longer have the option to withhold ISE-SARs from eGuardian that they submit to Shared Spaces.

PMO and FBI officials subsequently reached out to fusion centers regarding this issue—which included conference calls and formal correspondence—but the steps outlined above were not fully implemented.[29] The Director of the PMO explained that fusion centers own and operate Shared Spaces servers, and the PMO cannot compel them to share ISE-SARs with eGuardian. The director noted, however, that when fusion centers do not share SARs with eGuardian, they have other means to provide them to the FBI—such as e-mail or telephone. PMO officials added that some centers cited privacy concerns as the reason for not sharing with eGuardian, but they did not know the specific reasons why many fusion centers were not sharing at the time of our review. In its March 2013 letter commenting on a draft of this report, DOJ stated that it had made progress on this issue.[30]

Before this update on its progress, PMO officials stated that a total of 74 fusion centers had the capability to collect and share ISE-SARs, of which:

- Twenty-eight centers submitted ISE-SARs to both Shared Spaces and eGuardian in all cases.

- Twenty-three centers submitted ISE-SARs to Shared Spaces in all cases and to eGuardian on a case-by-case basis. Fusion centers that

---

[29]Correspondence to address the FBI's concerns included a message to fusion centers and other NSI stakeholders entitled, PMO, *A Call to Action: A Unified Message Regarding the Need to Support Suspicious Activity Reporting and Training* (April 2012).

[30]DOJ's written comments are reproduced in appendix VII.

do not submit ISE-SARs to eGuardian can provide them to the FBI through other means—such as telephone, fax, or email.

- Three centers were using Shared Spaces only to collect and share ISE-SARs and did not submit them to eGuardian. Executives and analysts from these centers said that they were concerned about their ability to remove ISE-SARs from eGuardian, which would be needed to be consistent with the fusion centers' privacy policies.[31] They noted that their fusion centers always provide ISE-SARs to the FBI, and do so through telephone or other means.

- Twenty centers were using eGuardian only to collect and share ISE-SARs and did not submit them directly into Shared Spaces, although ISE-SARs in eGuardian are forwarded to the FBI's Shared Spaces server and made available to users of Shared Spaces.

To help make fusion centers more comfortable with automatically providing ISE-SARs to eGuardian, the FBI has taken actions to provide users with additional controls over the ISE-SARs they submit to eGuardian. For example, the privacy policies at two fusion centers we contacted require ISE-SARs to be removed from systems when the information has no further value or meets criteria for removal. This differed from eGuardian's policy that, according to FBI officials, allowed for ISE-SARs that are found to have no nexus to terrorism to remain in eGuardian for 180 days.[32] Officials at 1 of these centers said that they were also concerned about the differing retention periods of ISE-SARs in Guardian and other FBI systems.[33] In response to similar concerns from a number of fusion centers, the FBI modified the retention period in Guardian to more closely mirror the 5-year retention period in eGuardian

---

[31]The Privacy Officer at a fourth fusion center said that his center was using Shared Spaces only to submit ISE-SARs at the time of our interviews. Subsequently, the official said the center received a legal opinion from the State Police that allows the center to simultaneously submit ISE-SARs to both systems.

[32]In commenting on a draft of this report, FBI officials noted that in February 2013, the FBI implemented a new feature in eGuardian that allows fusion centers to directly and electronically remove their ISE-SARs. ISE-SARs that are removed from eGuardian are still retained in Guardian and other FBI systems in accordance with their retention schedules. See appendix V for eGuardian and Guardian retention schedules.

[33]All SARs submitted to eGuardian are automatically sent to Guardian, which operates under different retention policies. See appendix V for eGuardian and Guardian SAR retention schedules.

and Shared Spaces, which the FBI believes addresses all fusion center concerns about retaining ISE-SARs.[34] Further, the FBI has created a feature within eGuardian that allows users to electronically submit SARs to the FBI without having them viewable to other users of eGuardian and Shared Spaces, which FBI officials said should address concerns about sharing personal information broadly.

The FBI's actions, implemented and planned, may address some of the concerns that fusion centers raised to us, but many centers still were not sharing all of their ISE-SARs with eGuardian at the time of our review. In addition, FBI officials noted that relying on telephone, fax, or e-mail versus automated means to share ISE-SARs introduces the risk that the FBI will not receive them. In our draft report that we provided to DOJ for comment, we noted that by reaching out to individual fusion centers to identify and address their specific concerns about entering ISE-SARs into eGuardian, the PMO and FBI could help ensure that the FBI will receive all ISE-SARs in a timely manner. In addition, establishing time frames to carry out these plans could improve accountability, as the PMO and FBI have previously committed to take similar steps but did not fully carry them out.

In its March 2013 letter commenting on a draft of this report, DOJ stated that since January 2013, an additional 21 fusion centers had begun to automatically share ISE-SARs with eGuardian. DOJ noted that of the remaining 7 fusion centers that were not automatically sharing ISE-SARs with eGuardian, 3 centers were submitting them electronically to eGuardian through other means, 1 center had temporarily suspended automatic submissions until a technical issue was corrected on their local server, 1 center had recently agreed to implement automatic sharing and was in the process of doing so, and 2 centers had identified legal issues that prevented them from adopting the automatic sharing solution. DOJ stated that PMO and FBI officials were involved in ongoing discussions with the leadership of the 2 fusion centers that raised legal concerns to identify what steps could be taken to mitigate those concerns.

---

[34]See, e.g., 28 C.F.R. §23.20(h) (providing that information contained in a criminal intelligence system operating through support under the Omnibus Crime Control and Safe Streets act of 1968, as amended, shall not be retained for longer than 5 years).

Automated Exchanges of ISE-SARs between Systems Have Not Been Fully Tested

The PMO and FBI have modified the technical capabilities of Shared Spaces and eGuardian to enable electronic exchanges of ISE-SARs between systems, but the entities have not tested the data exchanges in accordance with best practices for systems engineering. This has resulted in the systems being vulnerable to exchanging incomplete or inaccurate data. Specifically, the PMO and FBI have designed the technical solutions for the NSI so that (1) users that submit ISE-SARs to Shared Spaces have the option to simultaneously submit them to eGuardian and (2) ISE-SARs that are submitted to eGuardian are automatically forwarded to the FBI's eGuardian Shared Spaces server, and are therefore available in both systems. In addition, all ISE-SARs submitted to eGuardian are automatically made available to the FBI's Guardian system and will be routed to a JTTF. To accomplish this, SARs are necessarily transferred between eGuardian and Shared Spaces, and between eGuardian and Guardian, as shown in figure 3.

Figure 3: Suspicious Activity Report (SAR) Exchanges (Interoperability) among Shared Spaces, eGuardian, and Guardian

Mouse over system names or ⬤ on connecting lines for more information. For readers of print copies, see appendix VI.

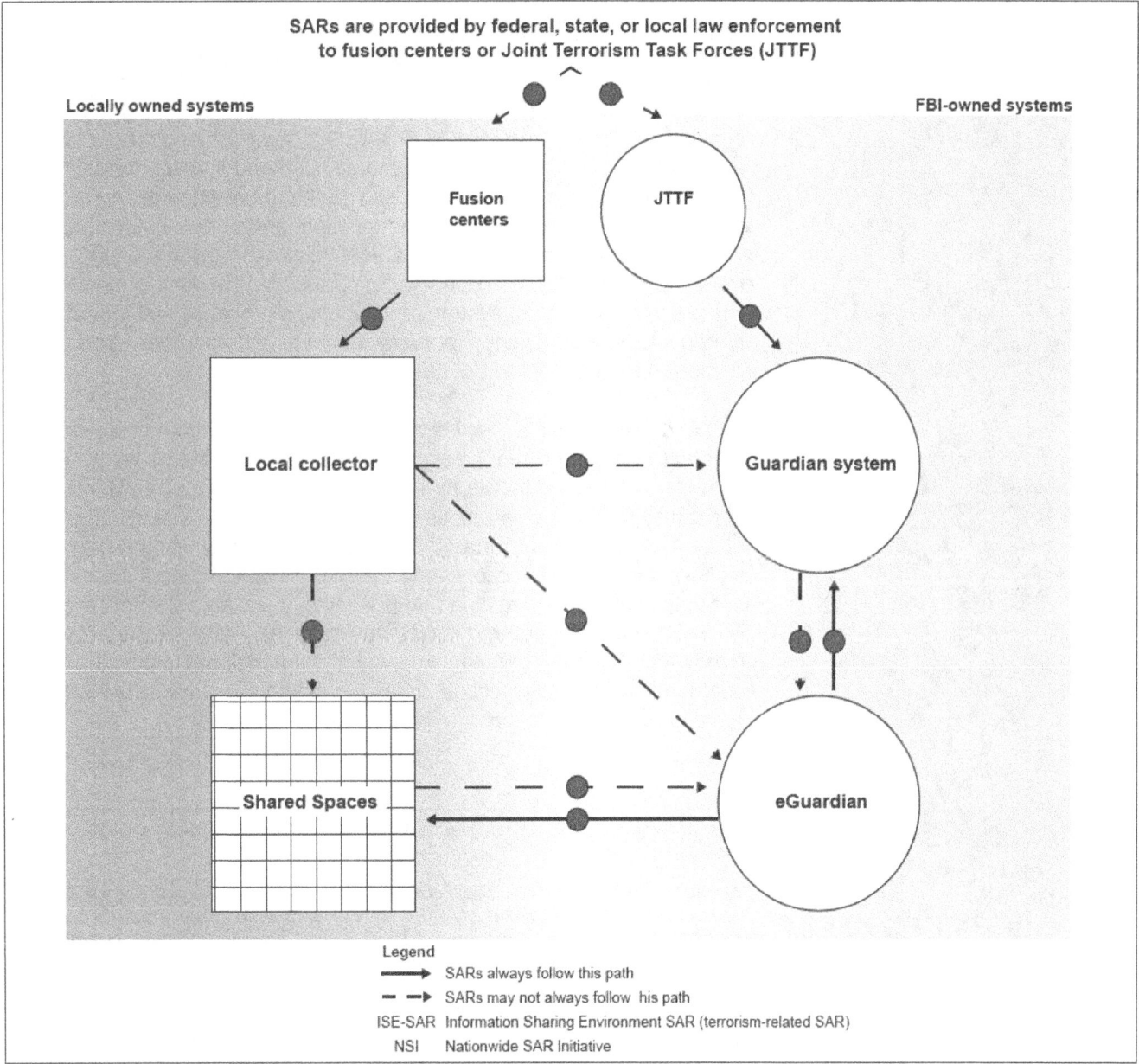

SARs are provided by federal, state, or local law enforcement to fusion centers or Joint Terrorism Task Forces (JTTF)

Locally owned systems

Fusion centers

JTTF

FBI-owned systems

Local collector

Guardian system

Shared Spaces

eGuardian

Legend
→ SARs always follow this path
– –► SARs may not always follow his path
ISE-SAR Information Sharing Environment SAR (terrorism-related SAR)
NSI Nationwide SAR Initiative

Source: GAO analysis of DOJ documents and interviews.

When agencies electronically interconnect systems, if the interconnection is not properly designed and tested, it exposes the systems to technical risks that the data processed, stored, and transmitted may not be complete or accurate. In order to mitigate these risks, agencies should follow best practices when developing systems. NSI stakeholders have taken steps to facilitate the exchange of data among NSI systems, including the development of the ISE-SAR Information Exchange Package Document, which provides NSI participants with common definitions of terms used in an ISE-SAR. However, among other things, best practices also call for agencies to develop and implement testing criteria and plans based on technical requirements—considering the cost and complexity of testing the interconnection, and the criticality of doing so to the agencies' missions.[35] Such testing would help to identify any errors that may occur when transferring data over the interconnection and storing it in the receiving system, and would help ensure that information entered into Shared Spaces remains complete and accurate when it is transferred to and stored in eGuardian.[36]

PMO and FBI officials acknowledged that they did not take these steps, but rather they performed "ad hoc" testing after the systems were connected, correcting problems as they came up.[37] FBI officials said they did not fully follow best practices when establishing the interconnection between eGuardian and Shared Spaces because they wanted to rapidly establish this interconnection—and they would rather accept the risks associated with ad hoc testing than the risks associated with not receiving ISE-SARs that were entered into Shared Spaces. Although such a trade-off may have initially been necessary, without additional testing in accordance with best practices, the FBI cannot know what ISE-SAR information it is not receiving or be assured of the accuracy of the

---

[35]See, for example, DOJ, *The Department of Justice Systems Development Life Cycle Guidance Document.*

[36]According to PMO and FBI officials, ISE-SARs are transmitted from an entity's local system to its Shared Spaces server, and then from its Shared Spaces server to eGuardian. The first interconnection—the initial push of ISE-SARs from a fusion center's local system to its Shared Spaces server—was beyond the scope of our review, but could still affect the quality of the data received by NSI stakeholders and would need to be factored into plans for performing interoperability measures going forward.

[37]The PMO later indicated that it had followed DOJ's *Systems Development Life Cycle Guidance,* but they were unable to provide any of the documentation that would necessarily result from doing so.

GAO-13-233 Suspicious Activity Reporting

information that it does receive, which could affect its related threat assessments and investigations.

Selected Stakeholders Reported Training to Date Generally Met Objectives, but Some Training Is behind Schedule and Has Not Been Fully Assessed

NSI stakeholders we interviewed generally reported that training to date fully or partially met objectives. The PMO has established mechanisms to assess the fusion center analyst training to help ensure that all analysts are receiving the information they need to participate in the NSI. However, the PMO has not assessed its line officer training. The PMO has provided training to about 290,000 of the 800,000 line officers; 2,000 analytical personnel; and executives at 77 fusion centers.[38] The PMO is behind schedule in providing training to the line officers and is taking actions to provide training to those officers who have not yet received the training.

Stakeholders We Interviewed Generally Reported That Training Enhanced Their Ability to Contribute to the NSI

NSI stakeholders we interviewed about training—including senior officials at 7 fusion centers, line officers at 4 local police departments, and analysts at 7 fusion centers—generally reported that the training fully or partially met all of its objectives or effectively focused on its target areas.[39] For example, fusion center executives we interviewed generally reported that the executive training—an in-person briefing provided to fusion center executives before they agree to join the NSI—effectively focused on the role of the executive in leading implementation and steps for conducting community outreach. Line officers generally reported that the line officer training—a 15-minute video available on DVD or online—increased their awareness of the NSI and helped them to recognize incidents that could lead to a terrorist act. For instance, one local law enforcement officer said that a scene in the line officer training of a routine traffic stop that revealed a person with fireworks and pipes in the car demonstrated the importance of officers assessing the totality of

---

[38]Line officers are law enforcement officers whose routine duties put them in a position to observe suspicious activity. Analytical personnel are officials from fusion centers and federal agencies that may have responsibilities to review SARs to determine if they have a nexus to terrorism. Executives are senior fusion center officials that are responsible for determining whether their fusion centers will participate in the NSI.

[39]Our work focused on executive, analyst, and line officer training that had been developed and rolled out to stakeholders for several years. Our work did not include the implementation of training to the private sector and homeland security partners that was just made available to stakeholders in April 2012.

information in a given situation to determine whether it should be documented as a terrorism-related ISE-SAR.

Also, the analysts we interviewed generally reported that the analyst training—an in-person 8-hour course—enhanced their ability to recognize terrorism-related SARs that they may not have identified as such prior to the training. Further, NSI stakeholders generally noted that the training enhanced their ability to avoid reporting SARs that are not terrorism-related. For example, an analyst from 1 fusion center said that the training helped clarify when an individual taking a picture or videotaping infrastructure is potentially terrorism-related and an ISE-SAR should be submitted versus a person taking pictures because the infrastructure is a tourist attraction. Finally, NSI stakeholders reported that the training enhanced analysts' or line officers' ability to protect privacy and civil liberties when vetting or documenting SARs.

PMO Assesses Analyst Training to Make Improvements but Does Not Assess Line Officer Training to Achieve Similar Benefits

The PMO has established mechanisms to obtain feedback on the training it provides to analysts at fusion centers and other agencies and uses this information to assess the training and make adjustments to improve it. Specifically, the PMO utilizes a survey to obtain written feedback on the training immediately following the training session, conducts assessments of participants' learning before and after the training, and obtains feedback on the training 90 days after it occurs. PMO survey results show that from January 2009 to July 2012, approximately 94 percent (1,273 of 1,342) of analysts rated the training as excellent or good and about 97 percent (1,279 of 1,316) reported that the training would help them apply the Functional Standard criteria to vet SARs.[40] The PMO also received input on how to further enhance the training, and incorporated suggestions. For instance, PMO officials reported that on the basis of this feedback, they adjusted the sequencing of the training segments and incorporated improved scenarios, using examples of actual ISE-SARs. This is consistent with factors we have previously reported that managers should consider when assessing agency training efforts.[41] One such factor is the collection of data corresponding to the established training objectives during the training's implementation, such as feedback on how

---

[40]The number of respondents differs because not all of those who took the survey answered all questions.

[41]GAO-04-546G.

well training programs are working and whether adjustments may be needed. Another factor is the use of appropriate analytical approaches to assess training, such as measures of training participants' reactions to, and satisfaction with, the training, or measures of changes in knowledge, skills, and abilities.

According to PMO officials, fusion center executives informally provide feedback both during the executive training and through interactions with PMO staff, which the officials said occurs frequently. They noted that the executive training is designed to provide an overview of the NSI and obtain the executive's agreement to participate in the initiative. Accordingly, PMO officials said that they assess the training based on whether the executives elect to participate in the NSI after receiving the training, and 74 of the 78 fusion centers are participating.

PMO officials said that they have not established a formal feedback mechanism for the line officer training, which could help ensure that the PMO's training provides the officers with sufficient information to enable them to identify and report terrorism-related suspicious activity that could help detect and prevent terrorist threats. This is because, according to PMO officials, the training is largely provided during routine agency roll call meetings in which many line officers view the training at one time, which makes it difficult for the PMO to ask the officers to complete a survey by hand or electronically. However, DHS has collected feedback through a one-page survey on some of its informational ISE-SAR materials that are meant to be distributed to law enforcement officers during roll call meetings.

According to PMO officials, line officers can also provide informal feedback on the training through the PMO's website. However, the line officer training does not include information that makes officers aware of this feedback option. Further, the website feedback mechanism does not include any specific questions about the training or how to improve it that would allow the PMO to assess or enhance it. Two of the online training providers have established their own feedback survey for line officers, and PMO officials said they review the survey responses. However, these surveys also do not ask specific questions related to the training objectives that would allow the PMO to determine how well the training is working or how to improve it. For example, the surveys only ask for a general rating of the content and do not ask questions that could help the PMO determine whether line officers have the information they need to perform their important role in identifying and reporting terrorism-related suspicious activity.

The officers from the five agencies we interviewed suggested that the training could provide information on current trends in terrorism, discuss the types of infrastructure and organizations that may be targeted by terrorists, specify what information should be included in an ISE-SAR, and include a quiz to test for understanding of the training materials, among other things. PMO officials said they planned to improve their efforts to review feedback on the line officer training, but they did not provide information on whether the PMO was going to solicit additional feedback or its approach for assessing the training. Taking additional steps to collect feedback from line officers could help the PMO improve its training to better help line officers fulfill their critical role in the NSI.

PMO Has Made Progress in Training Executives, Analysts, and Line Officers but Fell Short of Its Line Officer Goals; Stakeholders Are Taking Actions to Train More Officers

The PM-ISE has emphasized the importance of training executives, analysts, and line officers, and recommended that all agencies that participate in the NSI receive training. As of February 2013, the PMO had provided executive-level briefings to 77 of the 78 fusion centers and training to 2,000 analysts across the country. As most fusion centers are already participating in the NSI and have at least 1 analyst trained, PMO officials said that they are providing executive briefings and analyst trainings on an ongoing basis as needed to inform executives of NSI efforts and ensure that each fusion center continues to have at least 1 analyst trained.

As of February 2013, PMO data show that over 290,000 line officers had received training. However, this is about 64 percent short of the NSI's goal to train all line officers in the country (about 800,000) by the end of 2011. Officials from the PMO and organizations involved in developing the training—such as the International Association of Chiefs of Police—cited a number of challenges to providing this training. These include competing priorities of police departments, high turnover among line officers, difficulty reaching small and decentralized law enforcement entities, and the small number of PMO staff available to support training efforts. In addition, PMO officials explained that obtaining data on the number of line officers trained can be challenging, as they rely on police departments to report that number. The officials noted that the number reported is likely lower than the actual number of officers trained, although they acknowledged they have not reached all of the approximately 800,000 officers.

The PMO is taking actions to provide training to the remaining line officers. Specifically, PMO officials reported that they have been working with law enforcement entities to include the training as part of the entities' new officer training. PMO officials also said that they have worked with national law enforcement associations, such as the National Sheriffs' Association, to have the associations place a link to the line officer training on their websites. In addition, PMO officials reported that they have worked with the International Association of Chiefs of Police to reinvigorate the training efforts in five states, which, according to association officials, were chosen because of the relatively low percentage of officers that had completed the training, the presence of strong state police associations, and a large number of line officers. PMO officials said that they have seen an increase in the number of line officers trained in these states.

ISE-SARs Are Increasingly Being Used to Support Investigations and Analysis, but the PMO Is Not Measuring the Homeland Security Results Achieved

The PMO, FBI, and DHS have undertaken efforts to collect data on the number of ISE-SARs submitted, FBI investigations initiated based on ISE-SARs, and the potential usefulness of ISE-SARs in analyzing threat trends. These data show that NSI participants are increasingly using ISE-SARs, but do not track what difference the ISE-SARs have made, for example, in terms of their role in deterring terrorist activities or the number of arrests or convictions achieved. Such measures of results could provide decision makers with information on the program's impact on homeland security.

Available Data Show Stakeholders Have Increasingly Used the NSI to Investigate and Analyze ISE-SARs

Available data show that the number of ISE-SARs shared through the NSI and the number of FBI investigations based on ISE-SARs increased from fiscal years 2010 to 2012, and stakeholders have begun analyzing these ISE-SARs to identify patterns and trends posing security concerns. Specifically, according to PMO data, the number of ISE-SARs available to NSI participants in eGuardian and Shared Spaces has increased more than 750 percent from 3,256 in January 2010 to 27,855 in October 2012. According to PMO data, as of December 2012, the most frequent categories of suspicious activity reported were observation/surveillance; expressed or implied threat; sector-specific incident involving personnel, facilities, systems or functions; and theft/loss/diversion.[42] The number of

---

[42]See appendix II for additional information on the behaviors associated with each category of suspicious activity.

terrorism investigations the FBI initiated based on these ISE-SARs also increased by about 75 percent from fiscal years 2010 to 2012. According to FBI data, there have been more than 1,200 investigations initiated as of September 2012 (see fig. 4).[43]

Figure 4: Terrorism-Related Suspicious Activity Reports and Resulting FBI Investigations

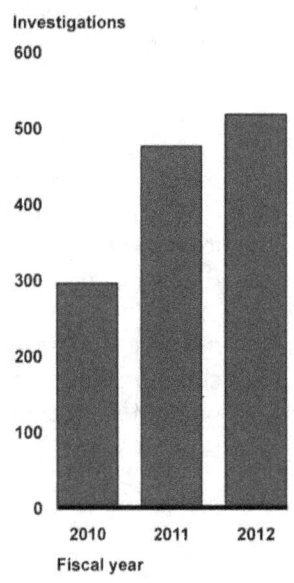

Information Sharing Environment Suspicious Activity Reports (ISE-SAR)

ISE-SARs (in thousands)

Date

ISE-SARs resulting in FBI investigations

Investigations

Fiscal year

Source: GAO analysis of PMO and FBI data.

Note: Fiscal year 2012 investigations include data from October 1, 2011, through September 8, 2012.

---

[43]According to FBI officials, the FBI reviews all SARs to determine if additional actions should be taken, such as a threat assessment or investigation. SARs that do not initially lead to an investigation may still have analytical value or provide useful information to help identify trends or provide context to other reported incidents.

According to FBI officials, in general, the data reflect growth of the NSI and enhanced support from federal, state, and local partners in identifying potentially terrorism-related activity. The FBI does not systematically track the number of ISE-SARs that have helped inform actions to deter terrorist threats or led to arrests or convictions because investigations are tracked in a different system and are not specifically linked to ISE-SARs. However, the FBI and PMO are anecdotally aware of some ISE-SARs that have led to arrests or enhanced already existing FBI investigations. For example, the 2011 NSI annual report includes information on an incident in July 2011 where two U.S. Marines reported that while they were traveling in a government vehicle in Seattle, Washington, a male motorist appeared to look at their vehicle's government license plate, and then attempted to run them off the road. The Marines reported the incident to their commanding officer, and the information was ultimately forwarded to the Washington State Fusion Center and the Seattle Division JTTF. The FBI had a related, existing investigation that showed the motorist had recently been in contact with an individual who was charged in a foiled Seattle terrorism plot in June 2011 to attack a Seattle military facility. The motorist was arrested in September 2011 and charged with assaulting the Marines.

DHS I&A has taken steps to determine the extent to which ISE-SARs could be or are used in analysis and found that most ISE-SARs reviewed contained information that could inform analysis and that NSI stakeholders are analyzing ISE-SARs to identify trends posing security concerns. For example, DHS I&A evaluated a sample of 3,044 ISE-SARs filed between January 2007 and December 2011 to determine the extent to which they were useful or had the potential for use in intelligence products, based on the ISE-SAR meeting the Functional Standard criteria, including information that would help identify a person or a location or address of the incident, or including a detailed description of the incident. I&A concluded that 69 percent of the ISE-SARs evaluated were useful or potentially useful, and found that the percentage of such ISE-SARs increased over time—from 66 percent in 2008 to 72 percent in 2011. PMO officials said that this analysis indicates that ISE-SARs shared through the NSI are of high quality and have analytic value.

DHS I&A also conducted a survey in April 2011 to determine the extent to which federal, state, local, tribal, and territorial agencies used ISE-SARs to develop analytical products. I&A found that in addition to the periodic products it develops, (1) the FBI, U.S. Coast Guard, Transportation Security Administration, and National Protection and Programs Directorate have developed ISE-SAR-based products, and (2) state, local, tribal, and territorial agencies have developed numerous products, the frequency and scope of which varied by region.[44] Such products included I&A's "Roll Call Releases," which use actual ISE-SARs to illustrate how agencies should apply the Functional Standard criteria, such as eliciting information on the purpose, operations, or security procedures of a facility that could be a potential target of a terrorist attack. Fusion centers have also developed products, such as the New Jersey Regional Operations Intelligence Center's quarterly reports, which identify trends in suspicious activity reporting in the state of New Jersey to help law enforcement focus resources on potential threats.

On the basis of the April 2011 survey results, I&A recommended that federal entities (1) provide additional support to fusion centers in regions with low analytical production and (2) increase the frequency of analytical products that focus on threats, such as threats to critical infrastructure, within specific geographic areas. In response, officials said I&A created the Field Analytic Support Taskforce in October 2012 to support state, local, and tribal intelligence requirements—including SARs—and facilitate regional collaboration among I&A analysts and federal interagency partners to identify, develop, and share intelligence products. PMO data show that ISE-SAR analysis may be increasing, as the number of Federated Search queries to review ISE-SAR data in Shared Spaces and eGuardian has increased from about 2,800 queries as of July 2010 to more than 71,000 queries as of February 2013.

PMO Has Not Established Plans or Time Frames for Implementing Measures That Assess the Homeland Security Benefits Derived from the NSI

The data above provide useful information on the outputs of the NSI, such as the number of ISE-SARs submitted and investigations initiated. However, they do not demonstrate results-oriented outcomes of ISE-SARs—such as the results of investigations or analysis, including arrests, convictions, or thwarted threats. Such information could help decision makers compare benefits achieved from investments in the NSI, and determine any needed changes to the process. In February 2010, the PM-ISE recommended that the PMO establish a performance measurement plan that includes a results-oriented approach and mature indicators that would provide information as to whether the ISE-SARs produced and shared under the program are meaningful and help achieve

---

[44]DHS I&A, *Survey of Analytic Production Incorporating Suspicious Activity Reporting* (Washington, D.C.: 2011).

the objective of ensuring the "dots are connected" as well as optimize resources and promote accountability.[45] The PMO has not yet developed such a plan or related performance measures that would allow it to assess the results and homeland security benefits of the NSI. PMO officials said that they are working with subject matter experts to fulfill the PM-ISE's recommendation and that the experts were trying to develop metrics aimed at measuring terrorism prevention. However, PMO officials noted that defining such measures was difficult and did not demonstrate what progress had been made in developing such measures. Further, the officials could not provide a time frame for completing the performance measurement plan because they could not ensure the consistent involvement of one of the requisite experts.

We have recognized and reported that it is difficult to develop performance measures that show how certain information-sharing efforts have affected homeland security.[46] However, we have also reported that some agencies have made significant progress toward establishing such measures. For example, in October 2012, we reported that DHS's U.S. Customs and Border Protection had established performance measures to help it assess its approach for identifying maritime cargo shipments that may contain terrorist weapons or other contraband for further examination.[47] We recommended that the agency further strengthen its performance measures by establishing targets to regularly assess effectiveness and DHS concurred. Standard practices for program management call for specific desired outcomes or results to be conceptualized and defined in the planning process as part of a road map, along with milestones.[48] Developing ways to measure results beyond the number of investigations or agencies performing analysis would help the PMO determine the extent to which the NSI is achieving

---

[45]PM-ISE, *Nationwide Suspicious Activity Reporting Initiative Status Report,* (Washington, D.C.: February 2010).

[46]See, for example, GAO, *Information Sharing: DHS Could Better Define How It Plans to Meet Its State and Local Mission and Improve Performance Accountability,* GAO-11-223 (Washington D.C.: Dec. 16, 2010), and *Aviation Security: A National Strategy and Other Actions Would Strengthen TSA's Efforts to Secure Commercial Airport Perimeters and Access Controls,* GAO-09-399 (Washington, D.C.: Sept. 30, 2009).

[47]GAO, *Supply Chain Security: CBP Needs to Conduct Regular Assessments of Its Cargo Targeting System,* GAO-13-9 (Washington, D.C.: Oct. 25, 2012).

[48]Project Management Institute, *The Standard for Program Management* ©.

intended results and identify needed improvements. In the approximately 3 years since the PM-ISE recommended that the PMO establish a performance management plan that includes a results-oriented approach and related measures, the PMO has not been able to demonstrate progress toward this goal. Without establishing plans and time frames for implementing measures, the PMO and PM-ISE lack a means for establishing accountability for ensuring measures are implemented.

Conclusions

Analyzing and disseminating terrorism-related information in a timely manner is critical to the government's efforts to detect and prevent terrorist attacks. The NSI is a key program to address information-sharing challenges and was designed to establish a nationwide capability to collect and share terrorism-related ISE-SARs among federal, state, and local law enforcement. Stakeholders generally reported that the NSI process is working well. However, formalizing mechanisms to provide stakeholders with feedback on the SARs they submit—which could include leveraging existing feedback mechanisms, such as those in eGuardian—and informing them of these mechanisms would be consistent with the PM-ISE recommendation and could help ensure that stakeholders receive the information they need to enforce SAR policies designed to protect privacy, maintain situational awareness, conduct accurate analyses, and motivate personnel to continue to report SARs.

Further, maintaining two systems to share ISE-SARs that provide duplicative services introduces risks identified by FBI officials that not all ISE-SAR information that should be shared is being shared or that the information that is shared remains complete and accurate when transferred between systems. The FBI and PMO have not identified the barriers that may prevent all ISE-SARs submitted to Shared Spaces from also being submitted to eGuardian or tested the interconnection between their respective systems to help ensure that the automatic exchange of ISE-SARs between the systems is complete and accurate. Without addressing these risks, the FBI cannot have reasonable assurance that it is receiving all ISE-SAR information that could help it investigate and prevent terrorist attacks. In addition, while the PMO assesses training for analysts and makes needed improvements based on assessment results, it has not developed or leveraged existing mechanisms to assess line officer training. Thus, the PMO lacks the ability to ensure that its training is effectively enabling line officers to perform their critical role in identifying and reporting on suspicious activities that may be related to terrorism. Finally, the PMO has taken steps to collect some data on the NSI. But until the PMO establishes a performance management plan that includes measures that assess what difference the ISE-SARs are making in terms of thwarting threats or resulting in arrests or convictions, for example, as well as plans and time frames for implementing the measures, the PMO and PM-ISE lack a means for establishing accountability for ensuring measures are implemented. Also, without such measures, decision makers cannot determine the extent to which the NSI is achieving intended homeland security results compared with investments made or identify and make needed improvements.

Recommendations for Executive Action

To help ensure that the NSI is effectively implemented and that investments are achieving desired results, we recommend that the PMO, in consultation with the PM-ISE, FBI, fusion centers, and other relevant stakeholders take the following three actions:

- implement formalized mechanisms as part of the NSI to provide stakeholders feedback on the SARs they submit, consistent with the PM-ISE recommendation, and inform stakeholders of these mechanisms;

- develop or enhance existing mechanisms to assess the line officer training in order to ensure that it meets training objectives and identify and make improvements; and

- establish plans and time frames for developing and implementing a performance management plan, including measures that assess what difference ISE-SARs are making and the homeland security results achieved.

To mitigate risks associated with having two systems for collecting and sharing ISE-SARs, we recommend that the Attorney General task the PMO and FBI to take the following two actions:

- identify individual fusion centers' concerns that prevent them from always submitting ISE-SARs to eGuardian consistent with the Deputy Attorney General's December 2011 memorandum, and establish steps to address these concerns—as well as time frames for implementing the steps; and

- develop and implement testing criteria and plans based on technical requirements, consistent with best practices—considering the cost and complexity of the testing, and criticality of the interconnection to the agencies' missions—to help ensure that the automatic exchange of data between Shared Spaces and eGuardian is complete and accurate.

Agency Comments and Our Evaluation

We provided a draft of this report for review and comment to DOJ, DHS, and the PM-ISE. DOJ and DHS provided written comments, which are reproduced in full in appendixes VII and VIII, respectively. DOJ agreed with all five recommendations and identified actions taken or planned to implement them.

DOJ agreed with the first recommendation, that the PMO implement formalized mechanisms as part of the NSI to provide stakeholders feedback on the SARs they submit and inform stakeholders of these mechanisms. DOJ stated that the FBI currently provides feedback to SAR submitters through the eGuardian system and noted that the PMO is working with the FBI to make this feedback available in Shared Spaces. In addition, DOJ stated that the PMO will help fusion centers develop mechanisms to provide feedback to the reporting agency. If fully implemented, DOJ's planned efforts will address the intent of this recommendation.

DOJ agreed with the second recommendation, that the PMO develop or enhance existing mechanisms to assess the line officer training. DOJ stated that it is taking steps to solicit feedback through the online version of the line officer training and may take additional steps, if funding is available. If fully implemented, DOJ's planned efforts will address the intent of this recommendation.

DOJ agreed with the third recommendation, that the PMO establish plans and time frames for developing and implementing a performance management plan, including measures that assess what difference ISE-SARs are making and homeland security results achieved. DOJ stated that the PMO will work with the FBI, PM-ISE, and DHS to identify such metrics and will reinvigorate efforts to measure terrorism prevention. The extent to which DOJ's planned actions will fully address the intent of this recommendation will not be known until the agency completes its plans and establishes time frames for implementing them. We will continue to monitor the PMO's efforts.

DOJ agreed with the fourth recommendation, that the Attorney General task the PMO and FBI to identify individual fusion centers' concerns that prevent them from always submitting ISE-SARs to eGuaridan and establish steps to address these concerns and time frames for implementing the steps. DOJ stated that since January 2013, an additional 21 fusion centers had begun automatically sharing ISE-SARs with eGuardian. DOJ noted that of the remaining 7 fusion centers that were not automatically sharing ISE-SARs with eGuardian, 3 centers were submitting them electronically to eGuardian through other means,1 center had temporarily suspended automatic submissions until a technical issue was corrected on their local server, 1 center had recently agreed to implement automatic sharing and was in the process of doing so, and 2 centers had identified legal issues that prevented them from adopting the automatic sharing solution. DOJ stated that PMO and FBI officials were involved in ongoing discussions with the leadership of the 2 fusion centers that raised legal concerns to identify what steps could be taken to mitigate those concerns. We recognize the significant progress the PMO and FBI have made in addressing this recommendation and will continue to monitor their progress in working with the remaining fusion centers to identify and address concerns.

DOJ agreed with the fifth recommendation, that the Attorney General task the PMO and FBI to develop and implement testing criteria and plans, consistent with best practices, to help ensure that the automatic exchange of data between Shared Spaces and eGuardian is complete and accurate. DOJ stated that the PMO and FBI are currently working together to develop a common understanding of the requirements for a formal, repeatable testing protocol. In addition, DOJ stated that the FBI plans to implement a technical solution by April 2013 to automatically notify the PMO when SARs that are submitted to Shared Spaces are not received by the FBI through eGuardian. If fully implemented, DOJ's planned efforts will address the intent of this recommendation.

DOJ, DHS, and the PM-ISE also provided technical comments, which we incorporated in the report as appropriate.

We are sending copies of this report to the Attorney General, Secretary of Homeland Security, Program Manager for the Information Sharing Environment, and appropriate congressional committees. This report is also available at no charge on GAO's web site at http://www.gao.gov.

If you or your staff have any questions about this report, please contact me at (202) 512-8777 or larencee@gao.gov. Key contributors to this report are acknowledged in appendix VII. Contact points for our Offices of Congressional Relations and Public Affairs may be found on the last page of this report.

Eileen R. Larence
Director
Homeland Security and Justice Issues

Congressional Requesters

The Honorable Thomas R. Carper
Chairman
The Honorable Tom A. Coburn, M.D.
Ranking Member
Committee on Homeland Security
   and Governmental Affairs
United States Senate

The Honorable Bennie Thompson
Ranking Member
Committee on Homeland Security
House of Representatives

The Honorable Peter T. King
Chairman
Subcommittee on Counterterrorism and Intelligence
Committee on Homeland Security
House of Representatives

The Honorable Susan Collins
United States Senate

Appendix I: Scope and Methodology

The objectives of this report were to evaluate (1) the progress federal agencies have made to implement the Nationwide Suspicious Activity Reporting Initiative (NSI), and what, challenges remain, if any; (2) the extent to which the technical means by which NSI stakeholders use to collect and share terrorism-related Suspicious Activity Reports (SAR) overlap or duplicate each other and introduce risks of these SARs not being shared; (3) the extent to which the NSI training has met its objectives, the NSI Program Management Office (PMO) is assessing the training, and the training has been completed; and (4) the extent to which the PMO has assessed how well the NSI is working and the homeland security results it has achieved.

To address these objectives, we reviewed NSI programmatic documents, such as the NSI concept of operations and annual reports, and obtained and analyzed Department of Justice (DOJ) data, including data regarding NSI implementation, training, costs, and results—from the inception of the PMO in fiscal years 2010 through 2012. We also interviewed officials from the Program Manager for the Information Sharing Environment (PM-ISE), DOJ, and the Department of Homeland Security (DHS) who are responsible for overseeing NSI efforts.[1] We obtained information from DOJ officials who manage the data about the steps taken to ensure their accuracy, and found the data to be sufficiently reliable for the purposes of this report.

In addition, to address the first three objectives, we interviewed nonprobability samples of officials from entities participating in the NSI, including officials from seven fusion centers—state- or locally- operated entities that serve as the focal point within a state or major urban area for sharing and analyzing threat information.[2] The seven fusion centers were the Boston Regional Intelligence Center, the Chicago Crime Prevention and Information Center, the Colorado Information Analysis Center, the Minnesota Joint Analysis Center, the New York State Intelligence Center, the Nevada Threat Analysis Center, and the Virginia Fusion Center.

---

[1]The PM-ISE plans for, oversees implementation of, and manages the government-wide Information Sharing Environment (ISE)—an approach for sharing terrorism-related information that may include any method deemed necessary and appropriate. See 6 U.S.C. § 485(a)(3), (f).

[2]Unlike a random sample, a nonprobability sample is more deliberatively chosen, meaning that some elements of the population being studied have either no chance or an unknown chance of being selected as part of the sample.

These fusion centers were selected based upon criteria designed to get a range of perspectives and experiences, which included geographic location, whether the center served an urban area, when the center received training, and level of participation in the NSI. To better understand concerns regarding the potential impact of the NSI on privacy, we selected four fusion centers that the PMO indicated had expressed some concerns with using eGuardian as a primary means of sharing SARs through the NSI. At each of the seven fusion centers, we interviewed executives—six of whom had received NSI training designed for executives—analysts who had received NSI analytical training, and officials who were familiar with their entities' systems for documenting and sharing SARs.

To address the first three objectives, we also interviewed a nonprobability sample of Federal Bureau of Investigation (FBI) officials who are responsible for investigating and analyzing terrorism-related SARs from seven field offices in the following locations that were proximal to the fusion centers we reviewed: Albany, New York; Boston, Massachusetts; Chicago, Illinois; Denver, Colorado; Minneapolis, Minnesota; Reno, Nevada; and Richmond, Virginia. When possible, we interviewed officials from local law enforcement agencies in proximity to the fusion centers we reviewed that had taken the line officer training. We met with officials from five local law enforcement agencies, including the Andover, Massachusetts, Police Department; Carson City, Nevada, Sheriff's Department; Highland Park, Illinois, Police Department; Minneapolis, Minnesota, Police Department; and the Norfolk, Virginia, Police Department. At all five law enforcement agencies, we met with officials who had taken the NSI training designed for line officers and who were responsible for reviewing SARs. To obtain perspectives from participating federal agencies, we met with officials from the Federal Protective Service and the Bureau of Alcohol, Tobacco, Firearms and Explosives, which were selected based upon having a relatively high number of officers who had received NSI training. Although the views of the individuals in our samples provide valuable insight into the implementation of the NSI, they are not generalizable to all federal, state, and local entities participating in the NSI. Other homeland security partners—such as critical infrastructure owners and operators, firefighters, and private security professionals—have begun to participate in the NSI. We did not include these entities in our work because their training just began in April 2012.

We took additional steps to address the second, third, and fourth objectives regarding NSI technology, training, and results, respectively.

To address the second question, we reviewed DOJ documentation regarding the two systems for collecting, sharing, and analyzing SARs, such as user manuals, implementation guides, and privacy impact assessments.[3] We compared the services of each system to determine the extent to which they overlap or duplicate and assessed the extent to which DOJ followed best practices for ensuring the systems effectively exchange information.[4] To address the third question, we reviewed and assessed PMO documentation regarding training objectives, targets, and recipient feedback mechanisms using leading practices for training programs.[5] To address the fourth question, we assessed the PMO's plans for measuring the results the NSI has achieved using best practices for program management.[6]

We conducted this performance audit from February 2012 to March 2013 in accordance with generally accepted government auditing standards. Those standards require that we plan and perform the audit to obtain sufficient, appropriate evidence to provide a reasonable basis for our findings and conclusions based on our audit objectives. We believe that the evidence we obtained provides a reasonable basis for our findings and conclusions based on our audit objectives.

---

[3]In general, the E-Government Act of 2002 mandates that federal agencies conduct privacy impact assessments to ensure sufficient protections for the privacy of personal information that may be collected, maintained, or disseminated using information technology. See Pub. L. No. 107-347, § 208, 116 Stat. 2899, 2921-23 (2002).

[4]See, DOJ, *The Department of Justice Systems Development Life Cycle Guidance Document* (Washington D.C.: January 2003).

[5]See, for example, GAO, *Human Capital: A Guide for Assessing Strategic Training and Development Efforts in the Federal Government,* GAO-04-546G (Washington D.C.: March 2004).

[6]The Project Management Institute, *The Standard for Program Management* ©.

Appendix II: Functional Standard Terrorism-Related SAR Criteria Guidance

The ISE-SAR Functional Standard was first issued by the Program Manager for the Information Sharing Environment in January 2008 and updated in May 2009, and defines common processes for collecting and sharing suspicious activity reports with a potential nexus to terrorism. Pursuant to a two-part process outlined in the Functional Standard, SARs that are determined to have a potential nexus to terrorism are known as ISE-SARs. The Functional Standard includes business rules and formats for exchanging ISE-SARs that were agreed to by both operating organizations (frontline law enforcement) and privacy and civil liberties advocacy groups. The Functional Standard has been designed to incorporate key elements that describe potential criminal activity associated with terrorism, as shown in table 3 below.

Table 3: Functional Standard ISE-SAR Criteria Guidance

Defined criminal activity and potential terrorism nexus activity	
Breach/attempted intrusion	Unauthorized personnel attempting to or actually entering a restricted area or protected site. Impersonation of authorized personnel (e.g., police/security, janitor).
Misrepresentation	Presenting false or misusing insignia, documents, or identification to misrepresent one's affiliation to cover possible illicit activity.
Theft/loss/diversion	Stealing or diverting something associated with a facility/infrastructure (e.g., badges, uniforms, identification, emergency vehicles, technology, or documents [classified or unclassified], which are proprietary to the facility).
Sabotage/tampering/ vandalism	Damaging, manipulating, or defacing part of a facility/infrastructure or protected site.
Cyber attack	Compromising, or attempting to compromise or disrupt an organization's information technology infrastructure.
Expressed or implied threat	Communicating a spoken or written threat to damage or compromise a facility/infrastructure.
Aviation activity	Operation of an aircraft in a manner that reasonably may be interpreted as suspicious, or posing a threat to people or property. Such operation may or may not be a violation of Federal Aviation Regulations.

Potential criminal or noncriminal activity requiring additional fact information during investigation[a]	
Eliciting information	Questioning individuals acting at a level beyond mere curiosity about particular facets of a facility's or building's purpose, operations, security procedures, and so forth that would arouse suspicion in a reasonable person.
Testing or probing of security	Deliberate interactions with, or challenges to, installations, personnel, or systems that reveal physical, personnel, or cyber security capabilities.
Recruiting	Building of operations teams and contacts, personnel data, banking data, or travel data.
Photography	Taking pictures or video of facilities, buildings, or infrastructure in a manner that would arouse suspicion in a reasonable person. Examples include taking pictures or video of infrequently used access points, personnel performing security functions (patrols, badge/vehicle checking), security-related equipment (perimeter fencing, security cameras), and so forth.
Observation/surveillance	Demonstrating unusual interest in facilities, buildings, or infrastructure beyond mere casual or professional (e.g., engineers') interest such that a reasonable person would consider the activity suspicious. Examples include observation through binoculars, taking notes, attempting to measure distances, and so forth.

Materials acquisition/storage	Acquisition or storage of unusual quantities of materials such as cell phones, pagers, fuel, chemicals, toxic materials, and timers, such that a reasonable person would suspect possible criminal activity.
Acquisition of expertise	Attempts to obtain or conduct training in security concepts, military weapons or tactics, or other unusual capabilities that would arouse suspicion in a reasonable person.
Weapons discovery	Discovery of unusual amounts of weapons or explosives that would arouse suspicion in a reasonable person.
Sector-specific incident	Actions associated with a characteristic of unique concern to specific sectors (such as the public health sector) with regard to their personnel, facilities, systems, or functions.

Source: Program Manager for the Information Sharing Environment, Functional Standard v. 1 5, Part B.

[a]These activities are generally First Amendment-protected activities and should not be reported in a SAR or ISE (terrorism)-SAR absent articulable facts and circumstances that support the source agency's suspicion that the behavior observed is not innocent, but rather reasonably indicative of criminal activity associated with terrorism, including evidence of pre-operational planning related to terrorism. Race, ethnicity, national origin, or religious affiliation should not be considered as factors that create suspicion (although these factors may be used as specific suspect descriptions).

Appendix III: Federal Agencies Participating in the NSI

As of November 2012, 53 federal agencies and over 300 Department of Defense (DOD) entities were participating in the NSI, according to the FBI.[1] Twenty-seven of these agencies are considered "NSI compliant" because they have met all NSI participation criteria, including receiving an executive-level briefing, entering into an agreement to participate in the NSI, establishing a SAR protocol, completing the frontline officer training and SAR analytic training, establishing a privacy policy, and obtaining an eGuardian account. The other 26 agencies are "NSI operational" and have met all of the above requirements, with the exception of completing the SAR analytical training. The compliant and operational agencies are listed below, along with their parent organizations, as applicable.

NSI Compliant:

Federal Bureau of Investigation (DOJ)
Bureau of Alcohol, Tobacco, Firearms and Explosives (DOJ)
U.S. Marshals Service (DOJ)
Drug Enforcement Agency (DOJ)
Bureau of Prisons (DOJ)
Office of Security Services (Department of Commerce)
National Park Service (Department of the Interior)
U.S. Park Police (Department of the Interior)
Treasury Inspector General for Tax Administration (Department of the Treasury)
Environmental Protection Agency
National Institutes of Health (Department of Health and Human Services)
Food and Drug Administration (Department of Health and Human Services)
National Aeronautics and Space Administration
Diplomatic Security Service (Department of State)
U.S. Agency for International Development
Federal Communications Commission
Government Printing Office
Office of Intelligence (Department of Energy)
Federal Air Marshal Service (DHS)

---

[1]The federal agencies participating in the NSI include independent federal agencies and government corporations. FBI officials did not provide a complete listing of participating DOD agencies. They explained that DOD is responsible for implementing the NSI within the department.

National Infrastructure Coordinating Center (DHS)
Federal Protective Service (DHS)
National Operations Center (DHS)
Federal Emergency Management Agency (DHS)
U.S. Customs and Border Protections (DHS)
U.S. Secret Service (DHS)
U.S. Immigration and Customs Enforcement (DHS)
U.S. Coast Guard (DHS)

Operational:

Nuclear Regulatory Commission (Department of Energy)
National Nuclear Security Administration (Department of Energy)
Office of Health Safety and Security (Department of Energy)
Bureau of Indian Affairs (Department of the Interior)
Bureau of Land Management (Department of the Interior)
Law Enforcement and Security Headquarters (Department of the Interior)
Bureau of Reclamation (Department of the Interior)
U.S. Fish and Wildlife Service (Department of the Interior)
U.S. Forest Service (Department of Agriculture)
National Zoological Park Police
Internal Revenue Service (Department of the Treasury)
U.S. Mint (Department of the Treasury)
U.S. Capitol Police
Office of Security Services (Department of Education)
Federal Investigative Services (Office of Personnel Management)
Federal Reserve Board
Office of Security and Emergency Management (Department of Labor)
U.S. Supreme Court
Inspector General (GAO)
Department of Veterans Affairs
Office of Security and Emergency Planning (Department of Housing and
Urban Development)
U.S. Postal Inspector Service
Federal Aviation Administration (Department of Transportation)
Special Services Police (Central Intelligence Agency)
Tennessee Valley Authority
Amtrak

Appendix IV: Similar and Unique Services Provided by Shared Spaces and eGuardian

This appendix corresponds with figure 2 in the report, which is an interactive figure. The table below contains the text that is not accessible to readers of print copies of this report.

Table 4: Similar Services Provided by Shared Spaces and eGuardian

Service provided by both	Shared Spaces implementation (pop-up box)	eGuardian implementation (pop-up box)
Access to submit ISE-SARs into nationwide network	Fusion centers and other entities with Shared Spaces servers have the ability to submit ISE-SARs into Shared Spaces.	The FBI allows all law enforcement entities across the country to create eGuardian accounts and submit ISE-SARs into eGuardian.
Access to review and analyze ISE-SARs others have submitted	Fusion centers and other entities with Shared Spaces servers have access to the Federated Search tool, which enables them to review and analyze ISE-SARs in Shared Spaces. Fusion center directors can allow local law enforcement entities to have access to the Federated Search also.	The FBI allows all law enforcement entities across the country to create eGuardian accounts and review and analyze ISE-SARs in eGuardian
Ability to share ISE-SAR information with the other system	Many ISE-SARs that are submitted to Shared Spaces are simultaneously submitted to eGuardian.	All ISE-SARs that are submitted to eGuardian are forwarded by the FBI to its Shared Spaces server, which is accessible to users of the Shared Spaces' Federated Search tool.
Search and analysis tools	Shared Spaces has several search and analysis features similar to those of eGuardian, and also has enhanced analytic capabilities, such as the ability to drill down and link common ISE-SAR elements.	eGuardian has several search and analysis features similar to those of Shared Spaces, and also allows users to generate exportable reports on a variety of ISE-SAR-related information.
Ability to submit ISE-SARs to FBI JTTFs and to Guardian (the FBI's classified counterterrorism incident management system)	When submitting ISE-SARs to Shared Spaces, users may also simultaneously send them to eGuardian, which then forwards the ISE-SARs to the appropriate JTTF and to Guardian.	All ISF-SARs submitted into eGuardian are automatically forwarded to the appropriate JTTF and to Guardian.
Ability to remove ISE-SARs from the NSI on demand	Shared Spaces enables ISE-SAR submitters to remove ISE-SARs at their discretion.	The FBI currently requires that ISE-SAR submitters contact the eGuardian help desk and request their ISE-SAR be removed; upon obtaining a reason for removal, the FBI will remove the ISE-SAR. The FBI is working on a feature that will make this process electronic.[a]

Source: GAO analysis of DOJ documents and interviews.

[a]In commenting on a draft of this report, FBI officials noted that in February 2013, the FBI implemented a new feature in eGuardian that allows fusion centers to directly and electronically remove their ISE-SARs.

Table 5: Unique Services Provided by Shared Spaces and eGuardian

Service provided by Shared Spaces	Service provided by eGuardian
Control over who can add information to ISE-SARs [pop-up box commentary as follows] Only original ISE-SAR submitters can add information to ISE-SARs.	Ability for users other than the original ISE-SAR submitter to supplement ISE-SAR information. [pop-up box commentary as follows] eGuardian allows users other than the original ISE-SAR submitter to "add notes" to ISE-SARs.
Control over who can download ISE-SARs [pop-up box commentary as follows] For privacy reasons, Shared Spaces does not allow users to download ISE-SARs, but the NSI PMO is working on a "virtual download" feature that will enable users to temporarily download ISE-SARs into a controlled space for purposes of analysis.	Ability to access FBI feedback on ISE-SARs. [pop-up box commentary as follows] eGuardian users are able to view the outcome of the FBI's threat assessment of the ISE-SAR they contributed, as well as access contact information for FBI personnel with knowledge of their ISE-SAR.
Greater control of the retention periods of ISE-SARs [pop-up box commentary as follows] Fusion centers cannot retain ISE-SARs beyond 5 years unless the information is revalidated. However, many fusion centers have established shorter retention periods.	Ability to download ISE-SARs [pop-up box commentary as follows] The FBI allows users to download ISE-SARs.
Ability to restrict certain data elements from broader view [pop-up box commentary as follows] Fusion centers and other entities with Shared Spaces servers can select which data elements they want to be accessible to other users.	Fixed retention schedules for ISE-SARs in eGuardian and Guardian [pop-up box commentary as follows] All ISE-SARs in eGuardian are retained for up to 5 years, unless the user removes the ISE-SAR. All ISE-SARs in eGuardian are also shared with Guardian, which has different retention policies. See appendix V for eGuardian and Guardian retention policies.
Ability to perform a Federated Search over all ISE-SARs in the NSI [pop-up box commentary as follows] Users of Shared Spaces have access to the Federated Search tool, which enables them to search among ISE-SARs located on all Shared Spaces servers across the country, including the FBI's Shared Spaces server.	Ability to share information with the FBI but not with other users of eGuardian or Shared Spaces. [pop-up box commentary as follows] eGuardian users have the ability to submit SARs or ISE-SARs directly to JTTFs and Guardian without sharing them more broadly with users of eGuardian or Shared Spaces
	Ability to request coordination with the FBI [pop-up box commentary as follows] eGuardian users may check a box indicating they would like the FBI to contact them before the FBI does any investigative work related to their submission.

Source: GAO analysis of DOJ documents and interviews.

Appendix V: SAR Retention Policies in the FBI's eGuardian and Guardian Systems

SAR retention schedules are based on the outcome of the FBI's threat assessments for each SAR. Some SARs do not receive threat assessments as they are for information only, and their retention schedule is 5 years in eGuardian. The following table shows the retention schedules of SARs based on the outcome of their threat assessments.

Table 6: Retention Schedules for SARs in the FBI's eGuardian and Guardian Systems

| FBI system | Outcome of FBI threat assessment | | |
	No nexus to terrorism	Inconclusive nexus to terrorism	Nexus to terrorism
eGuardian	Deleted after 180 days	Deleted after 5 years	Deleted after 5 years
	After deleted, retained in or by Guardian (see below) ACS/Sentinel (30 years) NARA	After deleted, retained in or by Guardian (see below) ACS/Sentinel (30 years) NARA	After deleted, retained in or by Guardian (see below) ACS/Sentinel (30 years) NARA
Guardian	Deleted after 5 Years	Deleted after 5 Years	Deleted after 5 Years
	If queried prior to deletion, then No change	If queried prior to deletion, then After 5 years, supervisor can view until 10 years, then deleted completely	If queried prior to deletion, then After 5 years, supervisor can view until 10 years, then deleted completely
	After deleted, retained in or by ACS/Sentinel (30 years) NARA	After deleted, retained in or by ACS/Sentinel (30 years) NARA	After deleted, retained in or by ACS/Sentinel (30 years) NARA

ACS: Automated Case Support system (the FBI's former cases management system)

Sentinel: The FBI's case support system they are transitioning to (FBI's current case management system)

NARA: National Archives Records Administration

Source: FBI.

Appendix VI: SAR Exchanges (Interoperability) among Shared Spaces, eGuardian, and Guardian

This appendix corresponds with figure 3 in the report, which is an interactive figure. The table below contains the text that is not accessible to readers of print copies of this report.

Table 7: SAR Exchanges (Interoperability) among Shared Spaces, eGuardian, and Guardian

Element of figure	Associated pop-up box
SARs are provided by federal, state, or local law enforcement to fusion centers or JTTFs	
Dotted line going from statement above to fusion centers	Law enforcement agencies may provide SARs to fusion centers by a variety of means, such as telephone or e-mail, or by using eGuardian (SARs submitted using eGuardian remain in "draft" status and are not yet submitted as ISE-SARs to the broader eGuardian user base).
Dotted line going from statement above to JTTFs	Law enforcement agencies may provide SARs to JTTFs by a variety of means, such as telephone or e-mail, or by using the "eGuardian Express" feature within eGuardian (this feature enables them to submit SARs directly to the FBI that are not viewable to other eGuardian users).
Fusion centers	Fusion centers serve as focal points within the state and local environment for the receipt, analysis, gathering, and sharing of threat-related information among the federal government and state, local, tribal, territorial, and private sector partners.
FBI JTTFs	The FBI has established JTTFs to investigate terrorism-related activity.
Solid line going from fusion centers to local collector	Upon receiving SARs from law enforcement, fusion center personnel enter them into their local collector.
Solid line going from FBI JTTF to Guardian system	Upon receiving SARs from law enforcement, JTTF personnel enter them into Guardian.
Local collector	Each fusion center has a local collector where it stores SARs. These collectors may include commercial products, legacy systems, the SAR Vetting Tool (a software application developed by the NSI), or eGuardian (agencies may use eGuardian to store their SARs without disseminating them more broadly).
Guardian system	Guardian is the FBI's classified counterterrorism incident management system.
Shared Spaces	Shared Spaces is a collection of similarly configured servers that are owned and located locally, across the country, and searchable through a common portal called the Federated Search.
eGuardian	eGuardian is the FBI's unclassified system for sharing ISE-SARs.
Dotted line going from local collector to Guardian system	Fusion Centers can use eGuardian "web services" to electronically forward ISE-SARs from their local collectors to eGuardian. If doing so is desired, users may choose the "eGuardian Express" feature, which will ensure ISE-SARs are provided to Guardian and the appropriate JTTF, but are not viewable in eGuardian.
Dotted line going from local collector to eGuardian and solid line going from eGuardian to Shared Spaces	Fusion centers can use eGuardian "web services" to electronically forward ISE-SARs from their local collectors to eGuardian. They can also submit ISE-SARs directly to eGuardian using eGuardian's web interface. All ISE-SARs submitted to eGuardian are forwarded to the FBI's Shared Spaces server, which is accessible to users of Shared Spaces.
Dotted line going from local collector to Shared Spaces and from Shared Spaces to eGuardian	From their local collectors, fusion centers can electronically submit ISE-SARs to Shared Spaces only, or, using the SAR Vetting Tool developed by the NSI, they can submit their ISE-SARs to both Shared Spaces and eGuardian. If they choose to submit them to both systems, the ISE-SARs go first to Shared Spaces and are then forwarded to eGuardian.
Dotted line going from Guardian system to eGuardian	After SARs have been entered into Guardian by FBI personnel, unclassified information is generally shared with eGuardian.

Element of figure	Associated pop-up box
Solid line going from eGuardian to Guardian system	All ISE-SARs submitted to eGuardian are shared with Guardian and the appropriate FBI JTTF.
Solid line going from eGuardian to Shared Spaces	All ISE-SARs in eGuardian are forwarded to the FBI's Shared Spaces server, and are accessible to users of Shared Spaces.

Source: GAO analysis of DOJ documents and interviews.

Appendix VII: Comments from the Department of Justice

U.S. Department of Justice

Washington, D.C. 20530

MAR – 1 2013

Ms. Eileen Larence
Director
Homeland Security and Justice Issues
Government Accountability Office
441 G Street, NW
Washington, DC 20548

Dear Ms. Larence:

Thank you for the opportunity to review and comment on the draft Government Accountability Office (GAO) report entitled, *"Information Sharing: Additional Actions Could Help Ensure That Efforts to Share Terrorism-Related Suspicious Activity Reports Are Effective"* (GAO-13-233). The Department of Justice (Department, DOJ) appreciates the work of the GAO and has carefully considered the findings and recommendations presented in GAO's draft report.

The Department established the Nationwide Suspicious Activity Reporting (SAR) Initiative (NSI) Program Management Office (NSI-PMO), within the Office of Justice Programs' Bureau of Justice Assistance (BJA) in March 2010. Since its establishment, the NSI-PMO has been working in partnership with the Federal Bureau of Investigation (FBI), the Program Manager for the Information Sharing Environment (PM-ISE), the Department of Homeland Security (DHS), and state, local, tribal, and territorial government partners to implement the standards, policies, processes, and technology necessary for law enforcement agencies to share suspicious activity reports that are potentially indicative of terrorism while ensuring the protection of privacy, civil rights, and civil liberties of all Americans. To date, implementation efforts have far outpaced original timelines of four to five years, with 74 fusion centers currently participating in the NSI, as of February 2013. The majority of these centers are able to immediately and seamlessly share SARs to both the NSI Federated Search (Shared Spaces), as well as with the FBI via the eGuardian system, ensuring that the FBI receives all SAR-related information for possible investigation.

Based on their findings, the draft GAO report contains five Recommendations for Executive Action to the DOJ, which are restated in bold text below and are followed by our response.

Ms. Eileen Larence   2

To help ensure that the NSI is effectively implemented and that investments are achieving
desired results, we recommend that the PMO, in consultation with the PM-ISE, FBI, fusion
centers, and other relevant stakeholders take the following three actions:

1.   Implement formalized mechanisms as part of the NSI to provide stakeholders
       feedback on the SARs they submit, consistent with the PM-ISE recommendation,
       and inform stakeholders of these mechanisms.

       The Department agrees with this Recommendation. The FBI currently provides feedback
       through the eGuardian system to inform a SAR provider when information submitted in a
       SAR is used to open an FBI investigation or assist in enhancing an existing FBI
       investigation. The NSI PMO is working with the FBI to develop a technical solution to
       expand this capability to port this feedback into the Shared Space. In addition, the NSI
       PMO will provide support to fusion centers to help them develop a feedback mechanism
       from the fusion center to the reporting agency / officer.

2.   Develop or enhance existing mechanisms to assess the line officer training in order
       to ensure that it meets training objectives and identify and make improvements.

       The Department agrees with this Recommendation. The NSI PMO has already taken
       steps to assess the line officer training, to include comprehension questions and
       information for feedback on the online version of the line officer training. In addition, if
       funding is available, the NSI PMO will explore the development of a standardized Peace
       Officer Standards and Training (POST) certified training, which would include the NSI
       line officer training. Because of the standards involved with obtaining POST training
       certification, this training would include comprehension questions and also provide a
       mechanism for officers to provide feedback.

3.   Establish plans and time frames for developing and implementing a performance
       management plan, including measures that assess what difference ISE-SARs are
       making and the homeland security results achieved.

       The Department agrees with this Recommendation. The NSI PMO will work with the
       FBI, PM-ISE, and DHS to identify metrics that can illustrate the impact of NSI on
       homeland security to supplement reporting of the number of investigations opened or
       enhanced. While the Department is in the early stages of exploring these possibilities,
       such metrics could possibly include items such as the type of cases opened and the
       longer-term disposition of cases. In addition, NSI PMO will explore distilling existing
       metrics to the SAR provider level to display a more granular breakdown of the currently
       compiled number of investigations opened or enhanced. Finally, the NSI PMO will also
       reinvigorate their previous efforts to measure prevention, which were put on hold due to
       limited funding.

Ms. Eileen Larence 3

To mitigate risks associated with having two systems for collecting and sharing ISE-SARs, we recommend that the Attorney General task the PMO and FBI to take the following two actions:

4. **Identify individual fusion centers' concerns that prevent them from always submitting ISE-SARs to eGuardian consistent with the Deputy Attorney General's December 2011 memorandum, and establish steps to address these concerns—as well as time frames for implementing the steps.**

    The Department agrees with this Recommendation. Since January 1, 2013, the auto-push function has been installed in 21 additional fusion centers. There are now only seven fusion centers that are not automatically pushing SARs to eGuardian. Of those seven, three are submitting the SARs electronically to eGuardian by alternate means; one center has temporarily suspended the automatic push until a technical issue is corrected on their local server; another center recently agreed to implement the automatic push and is in the process of doing so; and two centers have identified legal issues that prevent them from adopting the automatic push solution. OJP and FBI are involved in ongoing discussions with the leadership of the remaining two fusion centers that have raised legal concerns regarding sharing ISE-SAR information with the FBI electronically via eGuardian to determine what steps, if any, could be taken to mitigate those concerns.

5. **Develop and implement testing criteria and plans based on technical requirements, consistent with best practices—considering the cost and complexity of the testing, and criticality of the interconnection to the agencies' missions—to help ensure that the automatic exchange of data between Shared Spaces and eGuardian is complete and accurate.**

    The Department agrees with this Recommendation. The NSI PMO and the FBI Guardian Management Unit are currently working to develop a common understanding of what is needed to establish a formal process based on the Department's Software Development Life Cycle standards and a repeatable testing protocol. In addition, technical staff, responsible for the Shared Spaces and eGuardian systems, have recognized the need for a common dedicated hardware and software environment to improve joint interoperability testing, as well as diagnostic support and issue resolution to ensure that overall system availability is maintained at a high level.

    Further, the FBI has developed a web-based technical solution to notify the NSI PMO when SAR are pushed by fusion centers via the Shared Space are not received by the FBI, which triggers an immediate inquiry by the NSI PMO to troubleshoot the problem. This web-based solution is anticipated to be fully implemented by April 1, 2013. Currently this process is being tracked manually and the NSI-PMO generates a weekly dashboard which has identified only a few instances in which SAR were not received by the FBI. Once implemented, the web-based solution should prevent transmission failures of SAR from the Shared Spaces to eGuardian. However, with the complexity of the technology and the differences in the Shared Spaces and eGuardian systems, coordinated

Ms. Eileen Larence   4

efforts between the NSI PMO and the FBI are ongoing to ensure that all SAR reported by
NSI participants are forwarded to eGuardian accurately and expeditiously in the future.

If I may be of further assistance to you, please do not hesitate to contact me. Your staff may also
contact Richard Theis, Assistant Director, Audit Liaison Group on 202-307-0116.

Sincerely,

Lee J. Lofthus
Assistant Attorney General
 for Administration

cc: Tony West
        Acting Associate Attorney General
        Office of the Associate Attorney General

        Trisha Anderson
        Senior Counsel to the Deputy Attorney General
        Office of the Deputy Attorney General

        Andrew G. McCabe
        Assistant Director
        Counterterrorism Division
        Federal Bureau of Investigation

        Laura R. Ingber
        Section Chief, External Audit and Compliance Section
        Inspection Division
        Federal Bureau of Investigation

        Mary Lou Leary
        Acting Assistant Attorney General
        Office of Justice Programs

        James H. Burch, II
        Deputy Assistant Attorney General
         for Operations and Management
        Office of Justice Programs

        Denise O'Donnell
        Director
        Bureau of Justice Assistance
        Office of Justice Programs

Ms. Eileen Larence   5

cc: Maureen Henneberg
        Director
        Office of Audit, Assessment, and Management
        Office of Justice Programs

        Richard P. Theis
        Director, Audit Liaison Group
        Internal Review and Evaluation Office
        Justice Management Division

Appendix VIII: Comments for the Department of Homeland Security

U.S. Department of Homeland Security
Washington, DC 20528

Homeland
Security

February 26, 2013

Eileen R. Larence
Director, Homeland Security and Justice Issues
U.S. Government Accountability Office
441 G Street, NW
Washington, DC 20548

Re: Draft Report GAO-13-233, "INFORMATION SHARING: Additional Actions Could
     Help Ensure That Efforts to Share Terrorism-Related Suspicious Activity Reports Are
     Effective"

Dear Ms. Larence:

Thank you for the opportunity to review and comment on this draft report. The U.S. Department
of Homeland Security (DHS) appreciates the U.S. Government Accountability Office's work in
planning and conducting its review and issuing this report.

The Department is pleased to note GAO's recognition of DHS efforts to ensure continued
adherence to the Suspicious Activity Reporting (SAR) privacy protections and standards,
including supporting fusion centers in their self-initiated efforts to perform peer-to-peer privacy
audits. In addition, DHS appreciates the positive recognition of its efforts to determine the
extent to which Information Sharing Environment-SARs could be, or are used in analysis to
identify trends posing security concerns. We also noted the report does not contain any
recommendations specifically directed to DHS.

We look forward to continuing our dialogue with GAO and others to further enhance
understanding of how DHS and its many partners across the Federal Government, public and
private sectors, and communities across the country have built and strengthened a homeland
security enterprise to better mitigate and defend against dynamic threats, minimize risks, and
maximize the ability to respond to and recover from attacks and disasters of all kinds.

Again, thank you for the opportunity to review and comment on this draft report. Technical
comments were previously provided under separate cover. Please feel free to contact me if you
have any questions. We look forward to working with you in the future.

Sincerely,

Jim H. Crumpacker
Director
Departmental GAO-OIG Liaison Office

Appendix IX: GAO Contact and Staff Acknowledgments

GAO Contact	Eileen R. Larence, (202) 512-8777 or larencee@gao.gov
Staff Acknowledgments	In addition to the contact named above, Eric Erdman (Assistant Director), Lisa Humphrey, Jeff Jensen, Thomas Lombardi, Nick Marinos, Heather May, Amanda Miller, Karl Seifert, Maria Stattel, and Jill Verret made key contributions to the report.

GAO's Mission	The Government Accountability Office, the audit, evaluation, and investigative arm of Congress, exists to support Congress in meeting its constitutional responsibilities and to help improve the performance and accountability of the federal government for the American people. GAO examines the use of public funds; evaluates federal programs and policies; and provides analyses, recommendations, and other assistance to help Congress make informed oversight, policy, and funding decisions. GAO's commitment to good government is reflected in its core values of accountability, integrity, and reliability.
Obtaining Copies of GAO Reports and Testimony	The fastest and easiest way to obtain copies of GAO documents at no cost is through GAO's website (http://www.gao.gov). Each weekday afternoon, GAO posts on its website newly released reports, testimony, and correspondence. To have GAO e-mail you a list of newly posted products, go to http://www.gao.gov and select "E-mail Updates."
Order by Phone	The price of each GAO publication reflects GAO's actual cost of production and distribution and depends on the number of pages in the publication and whether the publication is printed in color or black and white. Pricing and ordering information is posted on GAO's website, http://www.gao.gov/ordering.htm. Place orders by calling (202) 512-6000, toll free (866) 801-7077, or TDD (202) 512-2537. Orders may be paid for using American Express, Discover Card, MasterCard, Visa, check, or money order. Call for additional information.
Connect with GAO	Connect with GAO on Facebook, Flickr, Twitter, and YouTube. Subscribe to our RSS Feeds or E-mail Updates. Listen to our Podcasts. Visit GAO on the web at www.gao.gov.
To Report Fraud, Waste, and Abuse in Federal Programs	Contact: Website: http://www.gao.gov/fraudnet/fraudnet.htm E-mail: fraudnet@gao.gov Automated answering system: (800) 424-5454 or (202) 512-7470
Congressional Relations	Katherine Siggerud, Managing Director, siggerudk@gao.gov, (202) 512-4400, U.S. Government Accountability Office, 441 G Street NW, Room 7125, Washington, DC 20548
Public Affairs	Chuck Young, Managing Director, youngc1@gao.gov, (202) 512-4800 U.S. Government Accountability Office, 441 G Street NW, Room 7149 Washington, DC 20548